Sail Racer

Jack Knights

Sail Racer

Drawings by John Batchelor

Seamark Series
editor Bruce Fraser

Adlard Coles Limited

Granada Publishing Limited
First published in Great Britain 1973 by Adlard Coles Limited
Frogmore, St Albans, Hertfordshire AL2 2NF and
3 Upper James Street London W1R 4BP

ISBN 0 229 98674 9
Printed in Great Britain by C. Tinling & Co. Ltd, Prescot and
London

Contents

Illustrations

Photographs

Drawings

1 Eye to Eye with Yourself

The racing of sailing boats is a sport of chance, though many writers try to prove it is not. You can shape and finish and polish a rudder blade till it is so kind to the water that its passage is hardly noticed; but if the rudder, and the boat attached to it, is in one place and the useful puff of wind happens to be in another, you might just as well be steering with a piece of board ripped from a packing case.

The irremovable element of chance – and thank goodness the chance is irremovable since if racing was only a matter of science and application then how dull and everyday the sport would be – paves the way for opportunism. Hardly any other sport is so prodigal with opportunities. Till the finishing line is finally crossed there are always chances of catching up and overtaking; Olympic medals have been many times won and lost on that very finishing line. This is one sport in which it is plain silly to give up at any stage, however soundly beaten you may look at the time. For sailing you could reword the old saying to read: 'While there's hope there's sport.'

And just as there are countless opportunities in every race, there are special opportunities for everybody in the fundamental choices about which type of racing should be undertaken.

No other sport offers such variety and scope. Not least of its blessings is that one can go on enjoying it into a ripe old age, in fact many retired people will tell you that they didn't really get to grips with the subject till their enforced leisure gave them the time for serious application.

Consider the almost limitless horizons. For the young animal there is the very physical business of managing a difficult, over-canvassed and underweight singlehanded dinghy. For the totally dedicated and unashamedly ambitious there is the lure of the Olympics. For the family man of limited means there are countless budget classes costing hardly more to run than a moped. For the intellectual there are the strict

1

One-Design classes of moderate performance and with keel-boats the engrossing problems posed by the International Offshore Rule for handicap racing. For the scientific there are the classes allowing latitude in hull form and sail plan. For the home handyman there are the many classes designed for easy home construction. For the sedate there are keelboats designed to be sailed from within. For the speed and thrill hungry there are the day-racing multihulls. For the challenging there are the long distance, trans-oceanic marathons. For the staunchly independent there are the long distance, trans-oceanic solo voyages. For those able and used to putting money to work there are such events as the Admiral's Cup and even the America's Cup. For those who wish some seafaring with their racing, who glory in overcoming the natural inclination of their bodies to seek rest and warmth and comfort, there is ocean racing in all its forms. For those whose desire for these things is qualified, there is passage racing.

Choice of boat

So I invite you to lie on Dr Knights' psychiatrist's couch and release your stream of consciousness. For without self-knowledge how are you to choose the type of yacht racing which will best match your special qualities and be hindered least by your particular failings?

This choice of yours is perhaps the most important bit of opportunism the sport offers. Far too many boat racers are unsuccessful simply because they are attempting what is, for them, the wrong kind of racing. They are barking up the wrong tree and unless they subconsciously glory in defeat (a not unknown paranoia) they would be happier in some other kind of boat, doing another kind of racing. Too many skippers in their late thirties and forties continue to race the Olympic Finn singlehander, convincing themselves that they still enjoy it as much as they did, but actually having a pretty rough time as, whenever the wind freshens, they are drubbed by the fitter youngsters. Freud would probably have said that their con-tinuance in the class is a yearning to hold on to their vanish-ing youth. In simpler terms they would find that a change to a class which was less demanding physically but more rewarding to tactical ability (a class such as the Tempest or Flying Fifteen) would give them much more real enjoyment while a change to a JOG mini ocean racer or Quarter Ton Cupper racing under the International Offshore Rule would open up whole new areas of enjoyment that they had not realised existed.

And be warned . . . modern yacht racing in common with every other competitive activity is becoming increasingly demanding. There is still as much room at the top but a great many more people are struggling upwards to get there and the pace, for some, is killing. What is needed is a realistic appraisal of your limitations, be they limits of enthusiasm, opportunity, spare time or money.

Racing is becoming increasingly stratified. The gulf between the ordinary weekend club sailor and the international campaigner is widening and will continue so. In offshore racing, the few leading skippers and crews who are able to ship their yachts around the world and build anew every two or three years are making matters difficult for Mr Average Man with his stock yacht and pals and possibly family as crew. The evidence for this is all around. Though the sport of yacht racing is spreading, the popularity of the Olympic classes is actually declining. This is because sailors are beginning to realise that unless they can go all the way with their racing, it would be better if they kept clear of these top classes where the cost of competition is inescapably greater and the time needed for training and participation irreducibly greater. The same holds true in cruiser yacht racing though the manifestations are different. Entries in the regular seasonal programme managed by the Royal Ocean Racing Club have tended to decline over the past six years. But competition in shorter, easier, more practical races organized by bodies such as the East Anglian Offshore Racing Association, and the Solent Points Championship run by the Solent Clubs Racing Association, is increasing greatly.

There is a tendency among some to reason that racing in all forms is getting prohibitively difficult and so perhaps they should steer clear of it altogether. But these are the faint hearted. Racing in one form or another can be practical for anybody. The difficult but vital matter is to decide which is most practical for *you*.

Crew or helmsman?

Consider another important question of psychology: not everyone will be happiest as skipper. Many, for countless reasons, will be happy to avoid the worries and responsibilities implicit with the job. One can carve for oneself a famous and rewarding career as a crewman, and though skippers are two a penny, truly great crews are as rare as hen's teeth. Imagine the great satisfaction to be derived from having some famous skipper come courting your services, hiding for once his own pride as he tries to win you over so that you can help him to further successes.

A forward hand on a Flying Dutchman or 505, with her stability so dependent on the crew's use of his trapeze and her speed so dependent upon his management of the spinnaker, can make at least as much difference as the skipper at the tiller. No dinghy of this type ever won a major event without good teamwork. In the same way, no offshore racer however superlatively designed, however comprehensive her wardrobe of sails, will ever win an important race unless the navigator has done his sums correctly.

Fine crews often make mediocre skippers. Great skippers hardly ever make good crews and if you are naturally the one you will not get nearly as much satisfaction and enjoyment from pretending to play the part of the other. This sounds straightforward enough on paper but in actuality it may be a great deal more difficult to make up your own mind as to what you are best at. Though we should know more about ourselves than anybody else, it is often difficult to differentiate between what we think and what is really true about ourselves.

Are you ingenious? Do you have a well equipped home workshop? If you can truthfully answer 'Yes' to each, then perhaps you should move on, passing all thoughts of a One Design class and stopping only on the squares marked 'Restricted Class' or perhaps 'International Offshore Rule'. Otherwise you may find yourself unduly and unhappily cribbed and confined in a class which prevents you from doing all the things that you *know* would make your boat go faster.

To the beginner one can make various helpful generalizations. Firstly, there is no doubt that the quickest and surest way to learn good boat handling and racing technique is in a dinghy. Because of its extra liveliness and quickness a dinghy will teach you more rapidly. Because of its great sensitivity it will be able to show you more clearly the difference between good and bad handling. Because of the shorter courses the boats in a dinghy race will stay more closely together, thus teaching tactics faster. It is difficult to think of any leading big yacht skippers who were able to get to the top without a dinghy background. Even Ted Heath served his time in a Snipe and Fireball. And if the truth be known the few at the top who apparently got there without this grounding make sure that their crews are made up of small boat experts.

Secondly, when choosing classes, put a tight rein on your natural desire to show your independence. Sailing has always been popular with people who hate to think of themselves as conformists. In large part they go afloat to escape from conformity. Yet good racing usually consists of a lot of different people battling it out in similar, and hence conformist boats. Only in this way can one discover who is the best. So you may well get the best racing by joining the commonest, most popular class. It is no good choosing the boat which pleases you most, only to find that it doesn't please anybody else. Your only alternative then is to race her in a handicap class and though this may suit many people best, it is not the best racing. Think of it this way: though your boat must conform, you can remain as different as you like. If confined to one area, select the class that is most popular there. If you have a choice of clubs and areas choose the class that is national in preference to the one that is merely local. If you are really keen and prepared to travel, choose an international class. Always go for officially sponsored as opposed to 'free enterprise' classes. In this way your racing stands the better chance of being well regulated, of prospering from year to year, while your boat will have the best resale value.

But bear in mind that the better the competition to which you aspire, the more expensive is going to be your sport.

Perhaps the first cost of the boat won't in itself be prohibitive, but if you are to give yourself a good chance of being in the running you will have to be prepared for more new sails, more gear revisions and replacements, and possibly a new boat more often.

Try to remember that the fun you will get from racing is in no way related to the size and expense of the boat you race. A large boat increases scope in some respects; you go further, take more people with you, make more of a splash, but on the other hand the standard of racing is quite likely to be lower, the worries and cares of ownership greater, the importance of good organization more important to success, the portability and hence the ease with which you can take part in overseas events, more difficult. There are many who will tell you that the smaller the boat the greater the sport, and if people were completely honest with themselves (are you still lying comfortably on that couch?) the need to race bigger yachts is closely linked with the yearning for status.

I am convinced that at the top level of competition character and psychological make-up are of paramount importance and though it is difficult if not impossible to change yourself, you are halfway home if you can only fully understand yourself. At the top level also, a high and usually pretty equal level of expertise may be assumed. Boats in a good fleet are usually pretty equal too in quality, equipment and tuning. Therefore the difference is the will of the men aboard, and the so-called 'killer instinct' is nothing more than an intense will to win. Very many top skippers and crews never have this and they suffer for the lack of it, though they continue to enjoy their racing just the same. In normal life it would in fact be an undesirable and possibly antisocial trait, manifesting itself in obstinacy, boorishness and self-righteousness. To be brutally honest, top level racing does tend to be antisocial; family and friends have to be sacrificed so that practice time and money

Close-up of Rodney Pattisson and one of his crews, Chris Davies. Pattisson won the 1968 and 1972 Olympic Gold medals, and won the world championships in 1968, 1969, 1970 and 1971 in the Flying Dutchman class. Note extremely thin mainsheet and tiny mainsheet block. In this shot he is playing the traveller adjustment line and not the sheet itself.

François Richard

for new gear may be obtained. Summer holidays have to be spent around the major events and some become so obsessive that they can hardly prevent themselves from thinking about their racing even when they are many miles from their boats. Today, with the spread of 'frostbite' winter racing and the practice of winter training in the Olympic classes, there is hardly an off season.

The so-necessary killer instinct is valuable even away from the boat because it ensures that racing plans do not have to be sacrificed to mere family and private life. Afloat it is vital if good starts are to be regularly seized, if bad luck and adverse winds are to be overcome, if places are to be snatched on the final leg of a course when others are tiring, if precious points are to be accumulated towards the end of a series. Now this killer instinct is born rather than made, but if you know that you lack it, you can at least take care to bully yourself into trying to make up for it by being more determined, more persistent. And you can do whatever is possible to whip up an active dislike for the opposition when afloat, sufficient to give you a real motive for wanting to beat them.

Presumably the completely adjusted person, the perfectly orientated being, has no competitive feeling at all, let alone a killer instinct. Western civilization has developed the spirit of competitiveness as if it were a positive virtue, and for those who cannot get enough of it during working hours the racing of sailing boats provides an excellent outlet for the excess.

The question of whether the chicken or the egg comes first is closely related to another psychological conundrum – do you need self confidence (not to say conceit) in order to win, or does victory breed self confidence? The truth is probably that one goes with the other, that a little initial success, possibly first coming as a real surprise, helps to boost self confidence to an extent that leads to further success, and so on. I think this is why youngsters tend to beat their elders and betters so often. Youngsters don't have the time, or even, sometimes, the intelligence for much thought or introspection. Lacking self doubt, they necessarily possess self confidence. Some people are naturally going to find self confidence more easily built up than others, but a little sailing practice and hard graft can do wonders here, for if you go out and practise more than others (few yet practise their racing nearly enough) and if you take more trouble to prepare your boat, you will possess the concrete knowledge that you have done more to deserve success than others and this is the surest foundation of self confidence.

It is only too easy, for instance, to build a hang-up about a weak part of your sailing technique. You might get to think, following a capsize or two, that you are no good at gybing. What you should then do is not hesitate and vacillate before all subsequent gybes (which will surely lead to further capsizes and a growth of your hang-up till it reaches monster proportions) but go out one windy day and lay the ghost that haunts you, once and for all, by gybing and gybing again and again, till you finally get it right.

So too with light weather ability. Some get to thinking that they will never be any good in light winds. They begin to fear the onset of light airs as if it were the Black Death. Eventually their tiller fingers feel semi-paralysed whenever there is no whistle in the rigging. The best solution is to practise and practise whenever the wind is light, to make sure that your boat is well equipped to make the most of light winds.

There is another way out of the hang-up – one can recruit a crew who is complementary, possessing in plenty the very psychological features one knows one lacks oneself. If the skipper is inclined to be strung up and over-wound, the crew should be easygoing and casual. If the skipper is, truth to tell, a little scared of big winds, then his crew should be a Viking, revelling in a blow.

So far we've not spared a thought for boats and how they sail, but all the same, I do believe we have started out on the right footing. Really, racing under sail isn't about boats at all but about people trying to get the better of other people. It starts and ends with this simple truth.

2   What Makes a Boat Tick?

Though yacht racing is essentially one person or group pitted against another, the weapons count, and any self-respecting fighter is going to want his weapons to be the most effective possible. Since a methodical approach is going to help you greatly in your racing, we will first consider racing boats in very general terms which apply to all types and classes. After that we can begin to specialize. Later it will be shown that different priorities (of tuning, sail trim and general technique) will apply to each class and that big mistakes may sometimes be made in trying to apply lessons learned in one class to another. All the same, there are several primal truths about what makes a boat go fast, and it is essential to know a little about them first: we will take the hull itself, then the appendages of fin, keel, centreboard and rudder, then weight, followed by stability, the sails and the rig which holds them up.

Hull shapes are history

One of the first things to realise about hull shape is that nearly all of what we know today was understood many years ago. New constructional techniques have enabled us to get away with shapes which were not practical seventy years ago, but any idea that hulls have undergone revolutions in shape in recent years is quite illusory, as reference to any old books on the subject will quickly reveal. In fact, hull design tends to run in fashions following measurement and rating,, which over-react to every major change in shape. In simple terms hull shape is the result of a compromise between strongly conflicting requirements. If simple speed, straight ahead through the water were the only consideration, sailing boat hulls would be shaped either like racing eight shells, tremendously long, slim and with semi-circular sections, or like speedboats – short and fat. The racing eight shape cuts head resistance to the absolute minimum. The

Reveille, one of the French Reve de Mer class and an excellent example of the smallest size offshore racer. Designed by Group Finot of Paris and built by Chantiers Mallard of La Rochelle, she swept the smallest cruiser class in Cowes Week 1972. Only 22 ft overall, she is a little small for Quarter Ton Cup size level racing (rating at around 17.4 ft IOR and not 18 ft, the Quarter Ton limit).

lines are so fine there is little wave-making – wave-making resistance being one of the great sources of resistance to headway. The other factor that slows boats is skin friction.

The powered speedboat with her strangely fat, squat hull, cheats both these obstacles by using her abundant power to lift out of the water until she is planing across the surface like a skimming pebble. Lightweight, powerful sailing craft behave this way in certain conditions so that to some extent they share these fat, squat features. But in practical terms even the highest performance sailboat must spend much of her time sailing in light airs, or tacking against the wind, when planing will not be possible. Therefore she has to sacrifice many of the easy planing features for the sake of all-round performance.

The self-evident fact that sailing craft look very unlike racing eights simply proves that minimizing resistance to straightforward headway is only one of many necessary considerations. A practical sailing boat must also resist the heeling tendency of the wind, must resist the related tendency of the wind to drive the boat sideways (leeway), and must usually be able to perform well in rough water. She must handle nimbly, turn quickly, and in most cases accommodate those who will sail aboard her in some degree of comfort. Looked at in these terms the racing eight is full of faults. To begin with, thanks to the extreme slimness and the semi-circular section, she will be able to offer hardly any resistance at all to the heeling tendency of the wind, acting through the sails.

Dinghy or keelboat

In modern sailing craft stability, as this anti-heel quality is called, is achieved in a number of ways which conflict directly with the qualities making for easy headway. The hull may be made very wide in proportion to its length. It is hardly

One of the 23 foot Cobra two-man keelboats designed by the author. Intended for cheap home-construction in plywood and glassfibre tape, hard chine, ultra light, and slim, the Cobra had the speed potential to beat the Ian Proctor-designed Tempest upon occasion but was not as practical, so the IYRU wisely chose the latter for its new class.

Gerard Beavais, Cahiers du Yachting

necessary to point out that the wide flat barge will be more stable than the long, narrow log or racing eight. We also know that barges tend to be slower than racing eights. Alternatively a heavy weight in the form of a ballast keel, usually of lead, may be suspended beneath the boat. This will make for a resistance to heel that increases with the angle of heel.

But of course ballast increases overall weight and weight slows a boat just as effectively as undue, barge-like, width. Another, more sophisticated method of providing stability is to use the live weight of the crew to hold the boat upright against the wind. Obviously the effectiveness of this will be directly proportional to the amount of total weight which is contributed by the crew, which is another way of saying it will only be effective in small boats.

Crew weight may be put to use in a number of more or less effective ways. The obvious one is for the crew to lean backwards over the windward rail, tucking their feet under special toestraps to prevent themselves falling over backwards into the water. The effectiveness of this will be increased if the hull and deck, where the crew are sitting, is made wide, while the width at the waterline is reduced. The lever effect or righting arm of this crew weight will be enhanced still further if one or more of the crew either clamber out over the weather rail and lie out on a plank, or planks, or if they lace themselves up into special harnesses that enable them to clip themselves onto trapeze wires and so be right outside with only the soles of their feet in contact with the boat.

A few modern racing classes – the Hornet is the best known, and the International 10 square metre Canoe – use such planks, known as sliding seats. They are arranged to slide easily from side to side so that when tacking or gybing they can be quickly switched across the boat. In recent years the trapeze system has emerged as the most popular way of maximizing

Contenders racing in Chichester Harbour. The Contender is a most exciting new singlehanded class designed by Australian Bob Miller, which because of its high performance and the challenge it sets its skipper surely deserves Olympic status. Unlike the older Finn design, the Contender emphasizes crew agility and dexterity more than sheer weight and stamina. She is at her spectacular best in firm steady breezes on open water.

Derek Rowe Ltd

crew weight leverage, and is now used on the Flying Dutchman, Tempest, 505, Fireball, 470, International 14, Osprey, Contender (singlehander) and many other classes. It would doubtless be used also on other classes such as the Dragon, Star and offshore racers were there not rules expressly banning it from these boats. The trapeze is lighter, cheaper, simpler and far more wieldy than the sliding seat. In light airs when it cannot be used, it is out of the way and leaves the interior of the boat completely clear. The trapeze (Peter Scott and Beecher Moore both claim its invention) is one of the ideas which has changed the shape of racing. For young enthusiasts it epitomises the essence of modern racing – its speed, special difficulties and excitement.

The multihull

A third way of achieving resistance to the heeling effect of the wind is the provision of a second matched hull, as on a catamaran, to give the craft a wide stance or base, or similarly in adding to a central hull a smaller float on either side, as in the trimaran. (There is a very rare species, the proa, which has one large hull and a single float on one side only, with a skipper and crew devoutly hoping they will never be caught aback.)

Multihulls (cats, tris and proas) are the fastest sailing craft of all, since their hulls, being shaped more like our prototype racing eight, make very small waves and create minimal skin friction. These craft will be dealt with in greater detail later. Multihulls do have disadvantages as well. For one thing stability is quite different from that of the ballasted keel boat in that it decreases abruptly after the angle of heel increases past a certain point. Therefore multihulls are capsizeable, and once capsized they are likely to be much more difficult to get upright again than the boat which relies for her stability on the disposition of live crew weight.

Experiments made over a century ago proved that the resistance of conventional hulls to forward motion increased so sharply with speed that maximum speed was strictly limited. Above this maximum, which is directly proportional to waterline length, the waves made by the driven hull are so large that it tends to fall into a kind of moving grave that it digs for itself. This speed (in knots) is usually reckoned to be roughly 1·34 times the square root of the LWL in feet. Very long, slim pencil shapes such as the racing eight and the catamaran hull are not inhibited in this way because they do not make nearly such large waves. The only escape from this limitation is by climbing out of the water and skating across its surface, and this requires a large driving force.

Importance of length

The ordinary kind of hull can only be made to go faster by increasing its length. This is why racing yacht classes are always based on length. The designer has the job of seeing to it that his creation approaches this maximum speed as easily as possible and as often as possible. For this reason he is sometimes tempted to increase width or beam, for by so doing he is increasing the resistance to heeling and so enabling more sail to be spread in higher wind speeds. But if he increases beam too much his boat will increase her wave-making and skin resistance to an unacceptable point; she will be particularly difficult in rough water, and she will become very difficult to steer, particularly when heeled. So there are severe practical limits to increase of width for the sake of stability or sail carrying power. Yet one of the most obvious developments in recent sailing craft design has been in the steady increase in beam to length ratios. This has happened not only in offshore racers, where the rating rules have always encouraged beam artificially, since it increases interior space and habitability, but in the dinghy and other small boat classes also. Very often the fattest boat of the year is also the fastest all-round boat of the year.

In one or two restricted classes such as the International 14 and Merlin Rocket, the growth of beam frightened the rule-makers so much that they imposed arbitrary maximum beam limitations. In much the same way, the arbiters of the IOR, the main offshore rating rule, are beginning to wonder aloud whether they should not impose curbs too. Meanwhile you can bet that next year's offshore designs will be a few inches wider for their length than were this year's.

17

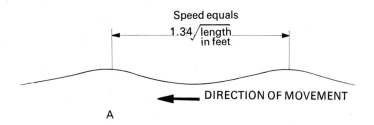

Speed equals

$$1.34 \sqrt{\frac{\text{length}}{\text{in feet}}}$$

← DIRECTION OF MOVEMENT

A

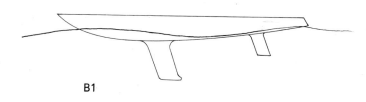

B1

B2

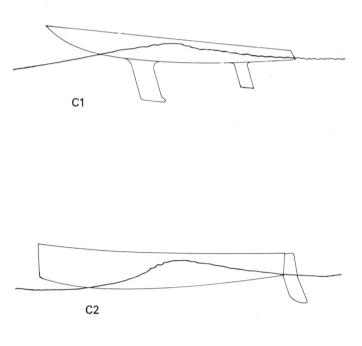

C1

C2

Length is the limiting factor in the speed of a boat because a moving hull makes one wave at the bow and another at the stern, and waves travel at a speed related to the distance between crests (A). This can be found from the formula: speed in knots = 1.34 $\sqrt{\text{Distance between crests in feet}}$. Hulls which have overhangs (B1) can push out their wave systems to increase their sailing length and will go faster than boats with vertical ends of the same nominal LWL (B2). The only escape from this limitation is a hull that is light enough and has enough drive to plane (C1 and C2). When planing the hull climbs up on the bow wave and out of the water, skimming along the surface, and the stern wave ceases to exist. With only the single bow wave, speed increases dramatically.

In lighter air and at slow speeds, wave-induced drag is negligible and skin friction on the area of wetted surface becomes the big factor. This is another reason yachts have overhangs at bow and stern – to diminish wetted surface in light weather, while still gaining the benefit of a longer wave system.

When we consider beam or width, we are thinking of the widest or fattest part of the boat. Another consideration which affects hull shape vitally is how far into the ends this fatness is drawn. One can have a fat boat which is pointed and fine in the ends, or a fairly slim boat which has proportionately much fuller, heavier ends.

Here again, the effects on speed and handling and all-round performance of these variables was pretty fully understood many years ago and it is only in reacting to rating and other design rules that designers follow apparent trends in one direction or the other. Thus the British, for reasons that have mostly been long forgotten, have been very suspicious of full-ended boats, much more suspicious than the Americans, for instance, (and also suspicious about too much beam, come to that) so that their design rules, as exemplified by the old Metre Rule and the old Royal Ocean Racing Club rule, deliberately encouraged designers to fine down their ends.

Because the new IOR rule could only come about with the agreement of all parties, it was a compromise between the British RORC and the Cruising Club of America rules, with the former's influence uppermost in the hull rules. Thus the encouragement of pinched-in ends continued though there are signs that the rule will be modified to aid the fuller bows and stern which the Americans have always preferred and which some recent tank-testing has shown to be theoretically better.

The wider stern

The trend in racing dinghies and other small craft has recently been toward fuller and wider sterns but fairly long, fine bows, with the forward waterlines almost straight. The wide flat stern

An International 14 ft dinghy, the senior high-performance class and the one which led to most of the others. Note large mainsail and low foretriangle encouraged by the design rules of this development class, which started in the late 20s and still flourishes in Britain and in parts of the USA and Canada. The class has produced some of the world's best small-boat sailors, but because of its short permitted overall length of 14 ft these boats will usually be beaten home by more modern classes such as the Flying Dutchman, 505 and Fireball. Their large sail area makes them exceptionally fast in light airs and their shortness gives the manoeuvrability needed on inland waters.

encourages planing, improves stability and enables the crew to be further aft, thus paving the way to still longer and straighter bow lines. This basically unbalanced shape is only effective if the boat is sailed flat. If allowed to heel unduly, so much rudder will be needed to hold her straight that speed will be lost. In larger and necessarily more balanced craft, bow shapes have recently tended to become fuller, just like sterns. But these full bows do suffer in a bad sea, throwing up more spray than finer, more flared forms and sometimes leading to undue pitching.

Most successful designs carry the basic character of the midship (or master) section right through the boat so that a veed boat is veed all through while a flat hulled boat is consistently flat or U-shaped.

A further trend towards filling out the ends and thus spreading the displacement is seen in the 'bustles' in the afterbodies of all new ocean racers of medium or heavy displacement. These are usually cunningly faired and moulded into the rudders. Not only do they tend to keep the stern wave further aft (thus reducing wave-making in this area), they also dampen pitching and enable the counter or stern itself to be divorced from, and smaller than, the true run or after shape of the boat. Thus they score under the measurement requirements since the all-important after girth measurements are smaller than they otherwise would be. When people talk of a high or low prismatic coefficient they are saying no more than that the yacht in question is comparatively full or fine-ended.

Weight and speed

The profile shape of the boat and particularly the line of the keel will always be closely related to the vessel's degree of displacement. Heavy displacement craft will necessarily be deeper than light displacement craft. Heavy displacement would be a thing of the past were it not for two influences: the rating rules under which keelboat classes are designed, and the need for interior space for accommodation in decked craft. Naturally, whenever a boat is fitted with a ballast keel she will have considerable weight or displacement, but if structural weights are pruned (as they can be with modern methods) the ballast can be chopped too, since it need only be a certain proportion of total weight. By saving weight in these areas and also in the rig a more easily driven hull is obtained. What results is the so-called light displacement boat that offers benefits of ease in handling, general seaworthiness (because lighter, she will tend to be more buoyant and dry), improved responsiveness to the helm and the potential for far higher maximum speeds (because shallower, finer hulls are less wave-making). Well designed, light displacement boats can be made to plane like powerboats and racing dinghies, even though they carry ballast keels.

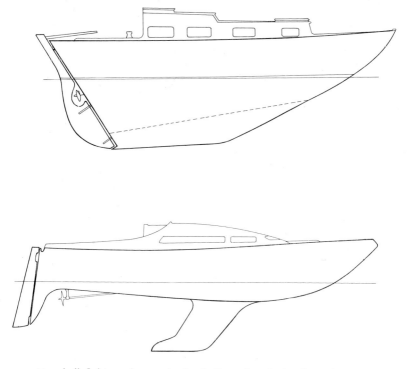

How hull fashions change: the South Coast One Design from Camper & Nicholson in 1955, a 21 ft waterline wooden cruiser-racer, rated well in her day and was fast for her rating, but now quite outclassed on rating by GRP boats of similar size, but with separate fin and skeg-hung rudder. The 22·25 ft waterline Nicholson 30, from the same designers in 1972, is a modern Half Ton Cup class boat. But the separate fin and rudder configuration is not new: boats of this type were racing before the turn of the century.

But the type is not allowed to develop, as it otherwise would, save in a few specialized one-design classes such as the Soling and Tempest, because the IOR and other rating rules discriminate against very light displacement. Also it is difficult to make a light displacement design as fast in light airs as a heavy one. The sail area to wetted surface area ratio is less favourable, and in light airs skin friction (also dependent upon wetted surface area) is more of a drag than wave-making.

In the same way, small boat racing classes are only as light as the rule makers consider they ought to be. Minimum weight limits are imposed because it is reasoned that otherwise boats would be constructed so lightly that they might break up in hard winds and, at best, have a limited life expectancy. These limits are arrived at by assessing the lightest boat which could be built from ordinary available materials.

Need for control

Perhaps it should be said and underlined, here and now, that the writer is firmly in favour of a policy of rigorous restriction and discipline in racing boats. Though some rules are bound to be unwise and retrogressive, the fact of having rules is a welcome and necessary safeguard that racing will not get beyond the pockets of people of average means. This is why so many can today enjoy racing sailing boats. And it is for the very lack of the same safeguards against the construction of highly developed, highly expensive, highly fragile racing cars that Mr Average Man has long since been forced off the racing tracks of the world and onto the grandstand benches.

It stands to reason that if a boat is to be raced mainly in light winds she can be given less beam, less flat hull sections and a less weighty keel. If prevailing conditions are fierce these features can be exaggerated. Earlier I pointed out that boat design is a matter of compromise on the conflicting requirements, and it is in the delicate proportioning of these requirements for given conditions within the framework of the class rules that the great boat emerges from among the merely good. The requirements themselves have all been well known for years.

24

The separate keel

So far we have been considering the hull shape without consideration of the appendages – keel, fin or centreboard, and rudder. In the immediate postwar years it was difficult to tell, in the case of the typical cruiser-racer, where the hull left off and the keel began. The hull served in part as the keel in resisting leeway, the sole purpose of the keel apart from holding the ballast. Today, and in spite of the rating rules, the keel has become much more sharply differentiated from the hull and it is now easier to see that it performs exactly the same function as the centreboard of a racing dinghy. In fact the change of rules which led to the deeply veed hull form and integral keel were only a reaction from the development of what were considered to be undesirably extreme types, at the end of the nineteenth century. These designs of almost a hundred years ago had the same deep, short, fin keels and flat, canoe hulls that are now apparently being produced by the IOR and which appear in the designs of modern racing keelboats, such as the Soling and Tempest and Flying Fifteen. The truth is that the fastest keelboats are the ones that look most like racing dinghies. One of the first to realise this was the Dutch designer Ricus Van de Stadt. Another was American Bill Lapworth and his compatriot Dick Carter, who was hugely successful because he realised that though the dinghy form was essentially faster, the rating rules favoured heavyish displacement. So with his first yacht *Rabbit,* he produced a very heavy dinghy, and with it won the classic Fastnet Race.

The fin keel scores in many ways. Firstly it functions more efficiently as a hydrofoil in countering leeway, even though it may only be a fraction of the area of the old, long integral hull-keel. It can be given a more efficient hydrodynamic section because it has a greater depth to width ratio (the two factors producing a high lift to drag ratio). Because the keel is small, wetted surface and hence skin friction are reduced. The short keel will also promote quicker turning.

One talks blithely about high aspect ratios, and certainly in the advanced small boat classes which permit experiment (the International 14, 505 and Fireball, for instance), centreboards have great depth compared to their width. They are still far deeper and narrower than the fin keels of larger racing yachts. However the most recent signs indicate that designers are beginning to experiment with slightly lower aspect ratios. For one thing, the deep narrow fin (assuming it carries no ballast) may hinder stability since it makes for a longer couple between the centre of lateral resistance of the immersed part of the hull and the centre of effort (or centre of area) of the sails. Secondly, a deep fin may well cause more drag than a shorter keel of the same area. Thirdly, there is the trend in the aircraft industry, as speeds increase, towards low aspect ratio wings and sweptback delta shapes.

In the late 1920s the Bavarian, Manfred Currey, produced a book on yacht racing which remains at least as comprehensive as any book on the subject published since. Possibly he went too far in comparing sailing boats with birds and aeroplane wings. There are big differences as well as great similarities. One is on safer ground when comparing sails with wings, but the behaviour of a fin as it cuts through water is in many ways very different from a wing as it moves through air. One can better compare the sailing craft's fin with wings of a supersonic plane, for at supersonic speeds air begins to behave rather as water does at boat speeds.

So if confused thinking about aerodynamics led us towards over-deep centreboards in our dinghies, lack of clear thinking of any kind in large yacht design has prevented keels, until recently, from being as deep as they should have been. But now this is being remedied, and it seems that in the coming years we will see fin keels and centreboards getting more and more similar in profile and sectional shape. Bear in mind, though, that the large yacht has practical difficulties in carrying an extra deep fin – she is more likely to run aground and more difficult to slip.

The best section

The aerodynamic confusion also extends to the sectional shapes of keels. These high lift aerofoils, with their bull noses and their maximum chord or thickness, one third back from the leading edge, may be all very fine when in the fresh air, but

26

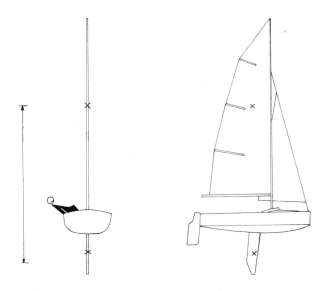

A slim, narrow centreboard or keel is theoretically more effective going to windward, partly because as the tip is comparatively smaller the pressure losses caused by tip vortices are proportionately reduced. But heeling moment and hence the difficulty of holding the boat upright is increased when a deep, theoretically efficient, board is used. Compare the length of the couple between the deep, narrow board and the high aspect ratio sail plan to the broader, shallower board and relatively low sail plan.

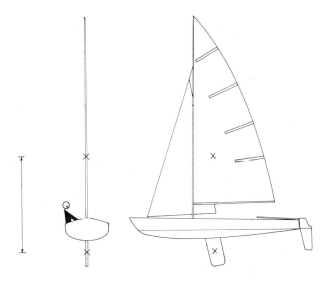

are perhaps, too fat for their own good, when knifing through deep water. Note that the foils of the new breed of powered hydrofoil craft have extremely sharp leading edges and crescent shape sections with the foils just as thin as they can be made without structural failure. Note also that the blades of powerboat propellors are as thin as possible and, incidentally, there is a very great difference between the shape of the airplane propellor and that of the boat propellor.

Though most of the theorists will tell you that centreboards formed of thin, flat plate will be infinitely less effective in resisting leeway than the thicker, aerodynamic form, in practice, the racing dinghies with plate type centreboards are very little different in performance to those with thicker, aerodynamic forms. The Tempest, probably the fastest keel-boat of all for her size, makes do with a flat plate. My own experiments with a very fat and aerodynamic centreboard in a singlehanded, prototype design helped form these views for me. That particular board did little or nothing to increase lift over drag, reduce leeway or do anything at all constructive.

If you follow my advice, your keels and rudder blades too will be considerably thinner than the aerodynamicists would want; the leading edge, while being blunter than the trailing edge and parabolic, will still have quite a sharp nose, while maximum thickness will be halfway, not one third back. Thickness in section, compared to fore and aft measurement should not be greater than one to twenty.

The rudder

Since rudders also help to prevent leeway as well as steer the boat (if the designer does not depend upon them for this purpose you can assume that his keel will be unnecessarily large), they should be shaped very much like fins and centre-boards, i.e. deeper in the water and quite narrow. If the helm is not to be heavy the rudder will need to be almost vertical with very little aft rake. Incidentally, one of the more fascinating considerations about keels is the amount of rake to give them. I have a theory that the thinner you make them, the less rake you need give them. Today's thinner keels are being given considerably less rake than yesterday's thicker ones. You can see this development in the recent work of the famous American designer Olin Stephens. Racing dinghy centreboards are usually arranged to be vertical when the boat is sailing in an average breeze, hard on the wind.

Rudders will work more efficiently and also be stronger, if fitted behind skegs. A skeg will enable a rudder to be turned

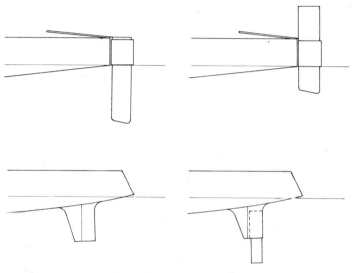

These modern rudder configurations are aimed at combining greater control and reduced wetted area, which is particularly important in light winds.

further without stalling. (Without a skeg the maximum turning angle will be found to be around 13 degrees). But no rudder should ever need to be turned much more than this for every degree is added drag. If a boat is difficult to steer and if the rudder is perhaps too small, its leading edge should be made blunt and more round than otherwise, for the increased snubbing will lessen the chance of the passing water separating, as it tries to turn through too abrupt an angle. But this roundness will necessarily increase resistance when the rudder is not being turned. I have evidence for this in experiments in the Tempest class. My boat went faster when a very snub rudder blade was sharpened, but I had to be more careful never to turn it too sharply.

In most boats, rudders can never be far enough aft . . . the further back the better and if the rules permit you to fit rudder hangings that get the blade back an extra inch or two, take full advantage of them. This will result in increased steadiness and increased obedience. It will increase the turning circle very slightly but a too tight circle would only slow the boat unduly as she turns. *The feather of an arrow is right at the back.*

The modern boat is, as has been previously explained, often of an unbalanced shape which means that in extremis it will often need firm handling if she is to go where she is pointed. The well balanced shape, as exemplified by the model yacht, which must be easily self-steered, is by no means the fastest shape. For this reason rudder blade area could with advantage, be increased, when hard pressed, (running under spinnaker, for instance). A retractable blade is easily arranged, either to retract into itself as in the case of a blade suspended under the stern of the boat, or to be withdrawn upwards in the case of a boat with a transom-hung rudder. One should note in passing that since rudders offer drag, those designers who rely over-much on model tank testing are inclined to give their creations rudders which are too small, practically speaking. Thus it comes about that almost every new Twelve Metre yacht designed in the last eight years has been better for having her rudder enlarged. The winner of the 1971 One Ton Cup was a standard design except that her rudder had been doubled in area (and extra ballast added – another modification which often works with modern stock designs).

Adjustable keels

Experiments in angling centreboards and fins to decrease leeway still further have been sporadic for the simple reason that results have been inconclusive. Perhaps the correct approach here is not to try to reduce leeway but instead, because lift is increased, to try to reduce fin area and accept the same leeway, hence gaining by reduced wetted surface and

30

lessened skin friction. There are of course big practical snags to be overcome before one can successfully pivot a heavy ballast keel fitted to an ocean racer. The American Dick Carter has the greatest experience here, but it is significant that his brother John Carter decided to lock his swing keel amidships for his second attempt at the Half Ton Cup with 'Crocodile'. Most successful skipper of a Carter swing keel boat is the German Hans Beilken with his latest Optimist, and he was one to follow the area reduction policy. Obviously it is easier to get a light centreboard to make an angle with the centreline and this can be done automatically. Yet it would be a rash observer to state positively that International 14s, Flying Dutchmen, 505s and Fireballs with swing (otherwise known as 'gybing' boards) consistently beat boats with boards that fit tightly into their cases.

It should be understood that we are talking here of very small angles of up to, but never more than, 3 degrees. Of course, there might be special times, (when not quite laying a weather mark, for instance) when it might be desirable to accept reduced headway in the hope of weathering the mark and so saving two tacks.

Trim tabs

Trim tabs on fins have gained much wider acceptance than swinging fins. For one thing they are much more easily fitted. It is significant that before the 1968 Olympics, the special centre-board which incorporated a trim tab, which Rodney Pattison had for his Flying Dutchman, was banned, but not before several of his rivals had dispatched urgent cables from the Olympic yachting venue at Acapulco, demanding that copies be made, post haste. Rodney had never actually used this trim tab board in any race and liked to say that its value lay in the unrest and panic it caused amongst his rivals.

Trim tabs are designed to perform a main and a secondary function. Their main job is to increase the efficiency of the fin by encouraging the water flow to cling to the keel longer. On every keel there is a breakaway point, perhaps half or two thirds distance aft from the leading edge, where the flow begins to

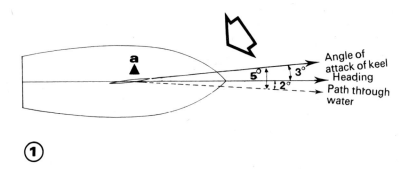

Angle of
attack of keel
Heading
Path through
water

①

Theory of the swing keel: sometimes a mechanically complicated ballast keel that can be rotated a few degrees under the hull is fitted to improve windward performance. The idea is that by swinging the front edge to windward (1) the lift of the keel is increased so much that leeway is all but removed and the course over the ground is the same as the heading. In practice it seems that it is not possible to eradicate leeway entirely without slowing the boat unduly, so it is better to use the increased lift to reduce keel area rather than leeway, giving the same lift to windward but a smaller wetted area and reduced skin friction.

It is easier to arrange for the centreboard in a dinghy to twist to windward, and angling or 'gybing' boards are often fitted (2). The slot is made wider, and the bolt is a slack fit in the board, so the front edge of the board can move from side to side, pivoting about point P, where protruberances are often attached to the board to control the pivot point and degree of twist. P is always made to fall aft of the main area of the plate, so the side pressure of the water from leeward (black arrows) makes the board take up the twist automatically. But even when very skilfully arranged and tuned, leeway is only minutely reduced, while the drag of the centreboard is much increased – partly due to the wider slot.

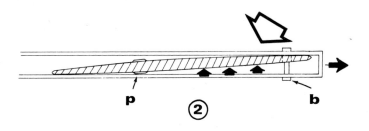

②

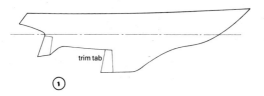

The trim tab (1) on a modern hull with separate skeg and rudder is intended to increase keel lift by making it assymetrical, and also to delay separation of the water flow over the keel (2, 3).

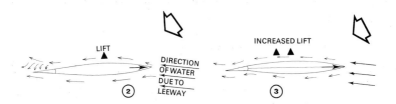

become turbulent. By delaying the onset of this turbulence the trim tab will lessen drag and improve lift. Therefore it should always be used when on the wind, blow high or low, but never at an angle of more than 3 degrees and rig up an alarm bell or other memory aid to ensure that the tab is re-adjusted every time the boat is tacked. (The latest IOR Mk III rule imposes a tax on trim tabs – good evidence that they work).

   The trim tab can also be put to good use in helping steering. Thus when hard pressed under an overlarge spinnaker on a tight reach, it can be made to share the load of the rudder and help prevent a broach. In the same way, in close manoeuvring it can, if so rigged, be linked with the tiller to improve close quarter handling and decrease the turning radius (but this is hardly of importance outside the specialized area of match racing as in the America's Cup).

   Trim tabs may become less common now that the latest IOR rating rule has imposed a tax on them. Cynics say that the longer you sail with trim tabs the less you use them so that they finally seize solid and then everyone is happy.

Weight

The first thing about weight is to echo the famous words of Uffa Fox: 'Weight is useful only to the designer of a steam-roller'. Weight is bound to increase displacement and thus the bulk of the hull which has to be pushed through the water. One can refine the shape of the increased bulk as carefully as one may, but increased drag will still accrue. Therefore reduce weight, everywhere and all the time. Your anti-weight campaign should be unceasing since every boat tends to gather weight as she goes through life – a characteristic not entirely unheard of in humankind. In the small boat classes never buy a boat which is significantly over the minimum weight permitted. In fact prefer to start out with an underweight boat which may be brought up to the rule, either by legal make-weights or extra heavy fittings. Even heavy displacement craft such as the Twelve Metre go better if made lighter. Here the weight saved may be splurged on extra lead ballast so that the ballast ratio may be improved allowing more sail to be carried (ballast ratios of the latest Twelve Metres are approaching an unbelievable 80 per cent, i.e. out of every ten tons of yacht, eight tons is in the form of lead in the keel). I have mentioned above that offshore racers often seem to be improved when extra weight is taken aboard. This may seem to run counter to the Uffa Fox axiom, but not really: in this specific instance the weight is used to sink the boat lower in the water, thus improving various depth measurements to obtain a more favourable rating, and permitting more sail to be carried for the same rating. Since stability is also increased with the extra weight, the extra sail can be carried to advantage. It is probably because designers are not yet fully aware how modern materials can reduce structural weight that they consistently design yachts which, when first launched, float well above their designed marks and hence need extra ballast.

Serge Maury, of France, winner of the 1972 Olympic Gold Medal in Finns, racing in hard wind. Note that he has moved well aft, even though hard on wind. His position is at least 1 ft aft of the main thwart. Long toe straps permit 80 per cent of body weight to be hung outside the boat. Note how wide the main boom is sheeted: this is only possible with a una rigged boat. Holes in transom rid boat of water quickly after capsize.

François Richard

Weight disposition

Rule 1 therefore is to reduce weight to the minimum. Rule 2 is to concentrate all unavoidable weight as low as possible and as centrally as possible in the boat. It is easy to see that an unduly heavy mast will raise the centre of gravity and therefore reduce righting effect or stability. Perhaps it is less obvious than an unduly heavy deck or unduly high free-board, or extra clumsy mainboom or extra large main halyard will all conspire to act in the same harmful way. All modern One Design classes built of fibreglass have elaborate construction rules to prevent the builder from making the bottom of the boat much thicker and heavier than the topsides and deck.

It isn't difficult to understand that a lower centre of gravity is better than a higher one (though there is a possible exception to this – when one is trying to make sails fill in a light wind and difficult sea. In these special circumstances a low centre of gravity or very high ballast ratio can lead to such a quick rolling period that the sails are prevented from filling and working because the boat rolls so fast the wind is shaken out of them. . . . The only thing to do then, if one is in an offshore racer, is to send a crewman up to the spreaders so that by artificially raising the centre of gravity, the roll can be dampened). Slightly more difficult to grasp is the fact that it undoubtedly pays to concentrate weights as centrally in the boat as possible, i.e. close to the centre of buoyancy and to reduce absolutely all superfluous weight in the ends of the craft.

Consider the hull as a seesaw, balanced about its centre of gravity. If the hull has heavy ends, it will, when made to pivot up and down in the seesaw manner, be found to do so slowly, deliberately and ponderously. If some of the same total weight is now moved into the middle, close to the pivot, the seesaw will now be found to have a much quicker, livelier lighter motion, whilst being considerably easier to stop. This quicker, livelier motion is what is needed in a sailing boat which must find its way over waves. Though you might think that a slow pitching moment would be better because it would give the boat more time to adapt herself to different waves, the practi-

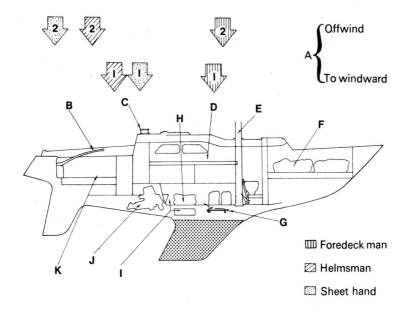

Weight distribution: this diagram of the She 27 Quarter Ton class cruiser-racer designed by Sparkman & Stephens shows the great trouble taken to concentrate weight as centrally as possible while racing. This will diminish pitching in a seaway, making the bow dip less and keeping the yacht drier. It will also enliven the steering responses. Crew should not regard the cockpit as their normal position going to windward, as it presses the stern down; they should only enter it for sail controlling purposes, the normal windward position being lying on a side deck – the weather deck for stability if the wind is strong, the lee deck to help the sails fill in light winds. Off-watch crews sleep in quarter berths abreast the cockpit or in the main saloon, never forward of the mast. The only exception is when the wind falls light but a big sea remains, when it may be necessary to spread out the weights fore and aft to slow the pitching rate.

Key

A Crew weight position: 1 to windward, 2 off the wind with spinnaker up
B Long tiller to encourage helmsman to sit well forward
C Sheet winches as far forward as practicable – cabin top may be suitable
D Spinnaker poles stowed abreast of cabin
E Mast well back from bow
F Sails and light stowage only forward of mast

G Anchor stowed low amidships aft of mast
H Inflatable dinghy stowed on cabin sole if carried while racing
I Heavy canned food and water carriers stowed amidships or under cabin sole
J Engine in saloon, not under cockpit, even though accommodation is impaired
K Long cockpit extends well forward

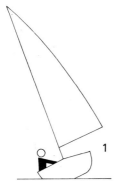

Trim: it pays to heel single sailed boats such as Finns, OKs and Moths to windward when running. This brings the centre of effort of the sail directly above the hull and helps steering (1).

In light airs, tacking, reaching and running, it helps to trim almost all boats down by the head (2). This immerses rounded forward sections of the hull while taking out of the water the flat after sections. In this way, wetted surface is minimized.

But in hard breezes it pays to move aft for beating, reaching and running (3). This increases stability, eases steering and controllability, keeps the boat drier, and prevents the bow running under.

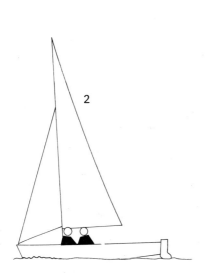

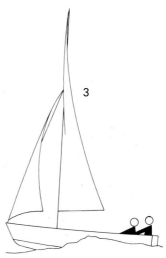

cal truth is otherwise. The boat with the quicker, livelier action finds her way over the waves better because, whilst reacting more quickly to each one, her ends are never as deeply immersed in any. Thus though she seems to be moving more than the boat with heavy ends, she is moving more lightly, staying drier and keeping her bow more consistently high, above the water.

You can see the same basic rule of gravity at work in the different business of motor racing. There is no doubt that the fastest cars around tight and winding tracks (and most modern tracks are tight and winding) are those with their weights concentrated most nearly in the middle. This is why engines were long ago taken from the front and put immediately behind the driver but ahead of the back wheels. In most cases, other weighty objects, such as cooling radiators, oil tanks and petrol tanks have also been shifted towards the centre. The driver has tended to be pushed towards the front for he is comparatively light. The result is a car which can change direction more easily. In the case of the boat the change of direction is on another axis and refers to the readiness with which the hull will adapt itself or change to the unevenness of the water flowing past it.

In small day racers where a large proportion of total weight is the live weight of the forward hand and skipper, the pair should always take care to see that they are as close together as possible. In ocean racers, designers have already persuaded owners to accept hardly any living accommodation forward of the mast. At the same time, cockpits are tending to be placed further in from the stern. In Twelve Metre yachts, most extreme of all, sail bins themselves are now being brought back aft of the mast and placed amidships.

As with the vertical centre of gravity, there will be some special conditions – when the sea is a great deal bigger than the wind would naturally make it – when this longitudinal weight concentration will have the reverse of the desired effect – giving an exaggerated pitching movement which won't give the sails a chance of getting down to work. When this happens it is simple for the crew to spread themselves as far forward and aft as possible. The only difficulty will be in deciding when these special conditions occur.

Maintaining shape – stiffness

I have reserved till last that other basic requirement of hulls, resistance to flexing, which is best thought of as structural rigidity or stiffness – not to be confused with stiffness in the stability sense – perhaps because least is understood about it and it is the most difficult to explain. The simple, practical truth is that a structurally stiff hull will go faster (in most conditions) than a less stiff one of otherwise similar characteristics.

For all manner of good reasons, wood is a less desirable boat building material than fibreglass. It is more expensive, more difficult to obtain in the correct qualities, it calls for more skilled hand work and afterwards requires much more careful maintenance. And yet in small boat classes of high performance where the choice of materials is optional, wood is still vastly more popular than glass – for the simple reason that it is stiffer, weight for weight.

At the time of writing, in spite of the advent of extra stiff sandwich foam lay ups and the like, wooden hulls still greatly outnumber fibreglass ones in the Fireball and Flying Dutchman class.

But this question of stiffness (which has little to do with strength) is more than a matter of wood versus fibreglass. There are indeed two separate aspects of the need for stiffness, one more easily comprehended than the other. A hull needs to be stiff if the rigging, and hence the rig, is to be under the necessary control. The rig imposes heavy loads on the hull. In its centre is the mast trying to drive itself down through the deck or keel in an effort to relieve itself of the wicked compression forces which are built up by the forestay, shrouds, backstay and kicking strap, halyards and sheets. All around the perimeter of the hull and particularly at bow and stern are the upward, tensional forces of these stays and shrouds. It takes no great imagination to see that if the hull is not as stiff as the proverbial girder, it will sag a bit under the mast, and curl up a bit at the bow, stern and around the decks where the shrouds are attached and in so doing, allow these stays and shrouds to slacken. As will be explained in a later chapter this slackness or sagging will play havoc with the efficiency of the rig. So it will need to be eliminated and therefore the hull will need to be as stiff as the stiffest girder.

Second, and more difficult is the stiffness needed to resist what might be called 'lost motion'. If the surface of the hull 'gives' as it meets the water or a wave, energy will be used up unnecessarily in forcing the hull back to its original shape, and this use of energy will sap the velocity of the boat. Each action of the sea and wind needs an equal and opposite reaction from the hull if things are to be kept in a state of equilibrium. If they are not, if the hull 'oilcans' or caves in, no matter how small the amount, the driving force will be decreased. I am very conscious at this juncture of being a layman, out of my depth in abstruse scientific problems, but I am not too worried if my explanation either baffles you or appears to counter the great eternal laws of our men of science. The fact is that a stiff hull will go faster than a floppy one and this extra efficiency will show itself to a greater extent in rough going than in smooth.

There are probably hydrodynamic, as well as mechanical reasons for this. If the hull yields in an area of high pressure, there will inevitably be a concavity. The water does not like to have to negotiate concavities and will tend to bridge the gap, causing an area of suction or low pressure, not to mention turbulence. This will be particularly harmful in the stern sections or 'run' of a small boat when planing. It is vital that this planing area be as stiff as possible.

If, as the bow crashes into a wave the hull allows itself to be nipped in, at the very moment of maximum impact there will be a loss of energy. As explained already, this can be decreased by concentrating weight amidships, so making the 'crash' lighter. But after one has saved weight forward as much as possible, there will still remain very large forces to be dealt with, and it is no good letting the hull cushion them by yielding.

It is easier to understand the same losses that may result from a too floppy rig. If, for instance, the top of the mast is allowed to whip or bow forward every time the bow hits a wave as it pitches forward, the pitching forces will be unnecessarily and wastefully accentuated. If every time an extra hard puff of wind hits the sails, the weather shroud stretches or the mast

41

bends, the sail will be allowed to sag and change its shape harmfully just when it should have been standing up to do its hardest work. So the chance of immediate acceleration will be lost.

The only time this 'give' or floppiness would be acceptable is when the boat is over-pressed with sail and staggering under it, so that she would actually go faster with less. At all other times hull and rig should be 'all of a piece', and the more of a piece they are, the more monolithic, the faster you will go.

3   The Rig

Before we get into rigs in any detail, we should pause moment-
arily to consider the very nature of sailing. Although I am
trying to be practical, addressing myself to practical people, a
theoretically based understanding of the subject will be helpful, particularly at a later stage when considering the complexi-
ties of tuning a boat for increased speed.

It is significant that though we sailors nowadays borrow
almost everything from aeronautics, the true reason for
flight was discovered by a man dealing with fluids, who
wrote a paper called 'Hydrodynamica'. The paper appeared
in 1738 and its author was a Swiss mathematician named
Daniel Bernoulli. The important part of this work, in so far
as it concerns flight through the air (which is, after all,
what a boat's sail is doing), is the explanation of how the
pressure of a moving fluid (or gas or air) changes with its
velocity.

If you nip a hose near its outlet the jet of water will reach
much farther. This is because the velocity of the water has been
speeded up by the constriction of the space through which the
water has to flow. In order that all the water from the
unconstricted part of the pipe can still flow through the
constricted part, the water has to increase its speed of flow.
This acceleration of flow also lowers the pressure of the fluid
acting upon the walls of the hose.

Now, in spite of what you may think, these facts, simple in
themselves and apparently in no way connected with sailing,
explain why a boat sails and a plane flies.

Compare a sail with the constricted hose, imagining the
hose sliced down its length and air replacing water. You now
have a hump over which the air must flow, and as it flows it is
made to increase its speed and hence reduce its pressure (you
can consider, if you like, that the air above it is limiting its
movement upwards, just as if it was the opposite wall of the
hose). So as the air moves over the hump, equivalent to the

upper surface of a wing or the leeward side of a sail, the air pressure is reduced.

Since the underside of an aerofoil is more or less straight, and the weather side of the sail is effectively straight because there is a dead patch of air in the belly, there is little tendency for the air on this side of wing or sail to accelerate and hence lower its pressure. Thus there is a state of disequilibrium – low pressure on one side and higher pressure on the other. This leads to what the layman thinks of as suction, and a natural tendency for the object (the wing or sail) to move towards the lowest pressure.

Now if we place the sail on a boat which has been made as resistant as possible to sideways movement by its keel and long narrow shape, we can begin to understand how a boat sails. The pressure differential causes suction at right angles to the sail. If the sail is pivoted at about 45 degrees to the centreline of the boat, as it would be if the boat were close reaching, it should be easy to see that by separating the components of this force there is a fair-sized resultant which is actually drawing the boat forwards through the water, even though the wind itself may be trying to push the boat more or less backwards (partly backwards, partly sideways).

This air-flow effect – which Bernoulli discovered back in 1738, over one hundred and sixty years before the first plane flew – is only part of the explanation of why a boat sails, but it is easily the most important part since it explains why a boat can be made to go against the wind. It is much easier to see that a boat can be bowled along with the wind, by the simple straightforward 'push' of wind on the weather side of the sail. In practice, sailing is a combination of Bernoulli's effect and simple old 'push', the exact proportions depending upon the course relative to the wind.

The Bernoulli effect shows itself in countless ways. If you loosely hold a spoon under a tap and allow the water to pour over the curved back of the spoon, the spoon will be sucked towards the water (instead of being pushed away from it, as you might expect). On a windy day, drying sheets pegged to a line will flap above the horizontal, being sucked upwards because of their curving shapes.

Rig and sails

'Rig' means all the sails, spars, wires and bits and pieces which help to make sails function efficiently. It is impossible to separate the sails from the rig because they are completely interdependent, but of course the rig is the slave of the sails. The sails are paramount and the job of the rig is to spread them effectively for the prevailing wind and sea conditions.

In later years there has been developed a new approach to sails and the way they are set. Not so long ago one carried around different suits of sails cut for light, medium and heavy conditions, then chose the ones that matched the weather best. But this was never quite as easy as it sounds. The weather does not like to be pigeonholed. No sooner have you decided that the wind is light than it freshens. And from minute to minute the average breeze may quite easily double its velocity and then halve it again. If you are sailing in a big sea, wind velocity is going to vary every time you climb on a crest and then descend into the partly sheltered trough.

What was needed was not two unused suits of sails in the fo'c'sle or in the car or back at the club, but a single suit of sails which could be made to cope with changing conditions and so become universally useful. The focus of rig development in the last fifteen years has been towards achieving this end, and this applies almost as much to large craft as to small.

At this stage, the innocent may stop to enquire why it should be necessary to match any sail to the conditions. 'A sail is a sail is a sail', they may think. But practical experience (even more than theory) says otherwise. In light winds a boat can effectively carry fuller, more deeply curved and hence more powerful sails than it can carry to advantage in fresh winds. Aerodynamicists should be able to understand this. A slow aeroplane is given a very fat, deep wing, using a high lift aerofoil section. High speed planes are profitably given much flatter, thinner sectioned wings in which more attention has been given to drag reduction than to the generation of maximum lift. Supersonic aircraft have the sharpest, thinnest wings of all. Now planes commonly fly at very steady cruising speeds, but the speed of sailing craft varies widely and depends entirely upon the strength of the wind. Since they never attain high

speeds as the aeroplane does they may be considered almost as stationary objects past which the wind flows at speeds which may vary twenty fold – from 2 knots to 40 knots for instance. If the sails are to be made to cope as effectively with a 2 knot zephyr as a 40 knot blast, they must be extremely adaptable.

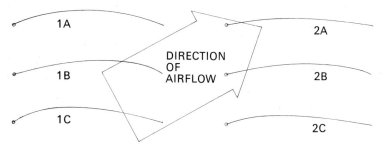

Flow in sails: 1A and 2A show full and flat sails with maximum arch at the mid-point, as recommended by Manfred Curry. But as the wind strengthens the sections become more like those in 1B and 2B. Since this is bad, creating drag and reducing the desired lift, it is better to start with the arch further forward, as in 1C and 2C.

The shape of sails

More and more, sails are being designed and cut to provide the maximum fullness needed for the lightest weather, while the rig is designed to provide progressive control over the shape of these sails so that they may be continuously flattened as the wind pipes up. Just as there is more than one way of building in the flow into the sail, there is also more than one way of taking it out again. In addition to the simpler question of how

Crown Prince Harald of Norway winning the 1972 Kiel Week Soling class from sixty of the best in the world. He is using American Melges sails. Note close sheeting of foresail (unlike many rivals, Harald does not use a self-tacking jib) and clewboard in foresail to give choice of sheet attachment positions (for fine adjustment of leech/foot tension). The mainsail Cunningham tack adjustment is hauled well home even though wind is only light. Note drooping main boom (denoting considerable mast rake) and central position of mainsheet on traveller. The lower shroud and upper shrouds are led to a single short length of track, with the lower shroud aft and upper forward.

François Richard

to take this flow away comes the no less important matter of countering the natural action of the wind in moving this flow into the wrong part of the sail.

Which raises the question of where this flow should be in a sail, in the first place. Manfred Currey, the great Bavarian sailor and theorist, devoted much thought to this matter back in the Twenties and made the fullest use of data given him by Germany's leading aerodynamicists of the period (particularly Professor Junkers, working at Dessau in 1923). This scholarly work cannot be improved upon today. All subsequent books on the subject have been but refinements and polishes.

Curry points out, first of all, that when sailing off the wind more fullness, i.e. a deeper curve, is advantageous. His polar curves, based on work by Eiffel, point to the fact that an arching of 1:7 (e.g. 1 foot depth of maximum curve where a sail is 7 feet wide) is best on a beam reach. But he is careful to point out that such an extreme depth will cause too much drag for optimum windward sailing, and he goes on to state that an arching of 1:13.5 will be best as an all-round proposition. Even then, he adds the caution that for very fresh winds, considerations of stability and weather helm may well lead to the need of flattening to about 1:27.

Of course the first conclusion to be drawn from all this is that one does indeed need different degrees of arching for different conditions.

On the vital question of where the maximum arching should be, Curry says simply that both his sailing experience and his and others' experiments have led him to believe that it doesn't really matter very much whether the maximum curve is well forward, as in an aeroplane's wing, or well back. He concludes that the best place is right in the middle of the sail, and makes the following point: 'My own experiments have confirmed what has been verified by experience, namely, that the position of the belly, whether forward or aft, is of little moment, and that under ordinary circumstances the sail is just as effective with the belly further aft, near the leech. The general opinion of sailors tends to the conclusion that it is most advantageous to have the belly in the fore-third of the sail, behind the mast. The construction of the bird's wing appears, indeed, to confirm this view, but still we should not forget that the bird has no mast in front of its wing, and the wind strikes the bird's wing at a somewhat smaller angle than it does the sail of a boat.' He continues:

'It is easy to imagine that the mast might counteract the favourable effect of the belly, if it lay in the fore-third of the sail, and it is certain that the belly, if too far forward, directly behind the mast, is harmful under all circumstances. Personally, I have obtained the best results with the belly about in the middle.'

The big jib

These are important words, coming as they do from the master in this business but two thoughts should be added. First, Curry was writing at a time before the genoa and masthead jibs were invented. He was thinking only of mainsails and had no idea that fifty years later the prime mover in an offshore racing yacht would be the sail ahead of the mast (which does not have the mast-induced drag of the main to contend with). Secondly he devoted no thought to the practical fact that as a wind freshens, the belly of a sail is moved inexorably further back in a sail. Therefore, unless it is put in the 'fore-third', as he calls it, it will inevitably end up much too far aft – and hence cause too much drag in a heavy breeze, when this would be fatal, and when maximum lift is not so vital.

Remember also that most of Curry's sailing was done in lake boats sporting fully battened mainsails. Though he was quick to see the aerodynamic advantages of full length battens over half a century ago, restrictive racing rules have prevented their application to conventional craft. Today they are only seen in special monohull classes and on multihulls.

Siting the curve

With these reservations, we should mark well the words of the master. The amount of arching does matter very much; the exact placing of it in the sail matters less. Though generalizations are dangerous, I will hazard one here: American sails

49

have always been cut with the flow farther aft in the sail than British sails. American racing yachts have more often beaten British yachts than the other way about. Is it to be wondered therefore that British sailmakers are at last beginning to move the belly further aft, towards (but never beyond) the mid-point?

This belly is built into a sail in two different ways. Firstly, the luff and foot of the sail are given a curve so that, when set on the straight edges of the mast and boom, they throw a fullness or belly back into the cloth. It may easily be seen that this puts the belly very close to the front and foot of the sail – too close for Manfred Curry.

The second, more sophisticated, difficult and subtle way, is to build the belly, panel by panel, into the whole sail by carefully shaping the seams. Just as a football may be made round by shaping its panels in a certain way, so a sail can be made very slightly round by shaping its panels very slightly. It is only a matter of fractions of an inch in certain panels, usually the ones near the bottom where the sail is widest.

Bending spars

The success or failure of a sail will hang upon these fractions of an inch. It may be seen that if the first kind of fullness – that given by the shape of the edges – needs to be removed from the sail, one only has to bend the spars so that they match the given shape and all the fullness is removed. More difficult is the matter of taking out the belly cut into the seams. If the spars are bent past the degree of curve cut into the edges, some shape is bound to be stretched from the body of the sail while other, harmful distortion will also occur, (there is more about bending spars in the chapter on tuning).

It will never be possible to remove all built-in panel belly, but much can be done by thoughtful adjustment of the tension of the edges of the sail. This will be dealt with in detail later but basically the principle is this: if one part of the sail, say the leading edge is stretched more than another, the belly will be brought towards that edge. With continued stretching the belly will be brought so close to the very edge itself that it can be thought of as having disappeared altogether, running into a harmless fold.

It was said earlier that the wind, as it freshens, does all it can to drag the belly of the sail further and further back towards the leech. This tendency is heightened by the fact that sheet tension is bound to increase as the wind increases. It is only natural that the sheets then have to be pulled in harder. But these act mainly on the after part of the sail and particularly up and down the leech. As I have just explained, tightening one edge of the sail has the effect of bringing the belly close to it. Now it can be seen that this will be harmful in the case of the necessarily tightened sheet since it will move the belly further back – something which practical experience teaches us is harmful. The only way of counteracting this hurtful effect is to tighten the luff of the sail still more, so that it remains comparatively tighter than the leech and the effect is to pull the belly forward, rather than backwards, in the sail.

In practice, in modern racing craft, sail belly is controlled by these two methods as the wind increases. The mast (and sometimes the boom) is bent to take out the belly given by edge shaping. The luff and foot tensions are progressively increased, not only to flatten the sail further but to keep the belly well forward, against the natural tendency of wind and increased sheet tension, to drag it further back.

Thus we are back to where we began this chapter, with the statement that sails and spars are completely interdependent, and that the spars are the slaves of the sails.

Interdependence applies also to the sails themselves. Only in a single-sail boat such as the Finn or Contender singlehanders is it possible to consider a sail in isolation. We know very well that the efficiency of a mainsail can actually be improved by setting a well placed, well cut foresail ahead of it. On the other hand, it may easily be greatly impaired by having a badly made and placed foresail to work behind.

The jib's task

As pointed out earlier, foresails or jibs (I use the words interchangeably in this context) may actually be more efficient

51

than mainsails because they do not have to work behind a drag-inducing, turbulence-generating mast. Their worth is further increased by their ability to improve flow over the mainsail by helping to smooth out the air that streams over the lee side of the main. In plan view, the foresail may be seen as a duct, combing out the wind before it meets the main. Aerodynamicists have long known the true value of a slot in the leading edge of an aeroplane's wing, either to increase lift by enabling the wind to bend through a larger angle over a thick, high lift wing, or to continue bending in a predetermined

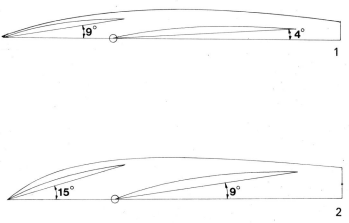

For ultimate closewindedness it has been found that the jibs of slim, efficient racing craft can be sheeted at angles of as little as 8 or 9 degrees to the centreline, with the mainsail closer still (1). But overlapping genoas call for wider angles, and short fat hulls will need wider angles in any case (2).

manner over a wing that is moving at decreased speed through the air – as when coming in to land – and so delay the critical 'stall'. A well placed jib can do very much the same thing for a mainsail, except of course that with soft sails the jib cannot impinge very much on the airflow either to speed it up or lower the pressure. This is one reason why fully battened sails, which withstand this impingement without flutter, should be more efficient than completely soft sails. But the jib of a conventional, soft-sailed boat does smooth out the turbulence of the flow past the lee side of the main, which would otherwise serve

52

to slow the flow, delaying the drop in pressure and also the lift. Thus a well placed jib will enable a boat to sail closer to the wind and faster. Tests with wool tufts have proved this to be so.

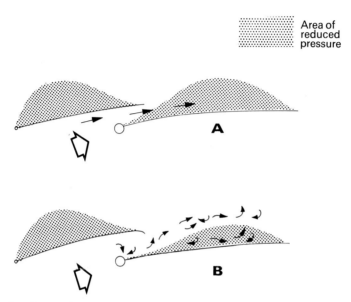

Area of reduced pressure

Jib and mainsail interaction should produce areas of reduced pressure approximately as at A, with speeded-up flow in the slot. A hook in the leech of the jib has a very bad effect on the flow in the slot (B), sharply cutting down the area of low pressure behind the main. A member of the crew standing or sitting in the slot can have the same effect.

The slot

This underlines the importance of the gap, space or slot, between jib and mainsail. Half the art of tuning the modern racing craft is in getting this slot just right for the prevailing conditions. Since more air is moving through the slot in heavy conditions, the slot will need to be large. If the slot is too small, a partial blockage will result. The mainsail will flutter and 'back' (the front of the sail tending to flap back and forth but always trying to move counter to the normal direction of the wind), the boat will be slow and heavy on the helm and generally have a constipated feeling – I think the word 'constipation' does indeed describe the symptoms exactly.

But since, as I have said, this slot question is one of tuning, it will be dealt with in greater detail later. As to the flow or fullness in jibs and its position, this too is very dependent upon the mainsail set behind it. Clearly, if the flow is too far back, the slot will be narrowed and the airflow hindered. It does seem as if, Manfred Curry notwithstanding, that the belly of a jib should be in the fore-third. Since one cannot bow the forestay forward as one can bow a mast, to flatten the belly, jibs are cut very much flatter than mainsails (the more so as the forestay will inevitably sag and hence increase the belly). The best control over the belly moving too far aft is halyard tension and the consequent luff tension. The rule here is, the harder the wind the tighter the luff. Once the peak of the sail is up against the sheave block at the hounds it is necessary to begin pulling down sailcloth from near the bottom (as with the mainsail). More and more skippers are using either adjustable jib halyards or tack downhauls or both. In offshore racing the so-called 'stretch luff' jib is becoming a *sine qua non* for all keen competitors.

While discussing the slot, let us consider for a moment the overlapping or genoa jib (so called because the great Swedish racing sailor Sven Salen first set an overlapping jib on his 6 Metre in January 1927, at the famous Genoa early season regatta). Salen invented the genoa jib, not because he was a great believer in Bernoulli's theories of speeding up airflow to lower pressure, but because he had found a way of setting unmeasured sail area. In the Metre classes in his day the triangular area of the mainsail was measured (leaving out the curved roach in the leech) plus a proportion of the fore-triangle. So already jibs were measured less severely than mainsails and were thus encouraged to get bigger and bigger (by moving the mast further and further aft). But the keen Salen saw that one could take the clew of the jib much further back than the mast itself, sheeting the sail somewhere near amidships on the lee rail. Tacking would be a little more difficult, but think of the extra, unmeasured sail area. From January 1927, yacht racing was never the same. Others seized on the genoa idea and ruthlessly developed it. Genoas themselves got bigger and bigger. It wasn't long before the yachts were being designed to suit the new sails, by being generally bigger and more powerful, with particularly powerful 'shoulders' in way of the mast. In all classes which allow them, the genoa is now the rule and even in some One Design classes, where every inch of actual sail area is measured, genoa jibs were incorporated. Thus the Dragon, when it was given a more modern rig, was endowed with a genoa, while the early Flying Dutchman, seeking extra speed after a less than convincing debut at trials to pick a new two man centre-boarder, was also given a genoa as the quickest, cheapest way of increasing sail area. Other, later classes, such as the 5.5 Metre, have had to resist continued attempts to have a genoa thrust upon them, while some, such as the GP 14 dinghy, have had one given them willy-nilly. All offshore racers have them, for it would be completely daft of a designer, reading the rules, to design a boat without them. As with the original Metre class boats, the offshore racers only have their foretriangles measured so that the headsail area which extends aft of the mast is excluded. In fact, were it not for the fact that the IOR insists upon a minimum size of mainsail, the latter might have disappeared altogether.

The genoa is nowadays so common that yachts without them are often said to look old fashioned. Yet the fact remains that it is nothing but a rule cheating device. Though it certainly creates a long slot between headsail and main, which is very difficult to tune well, the genoa was certainly not designed in order to improve flow over the lee side of the mainsail or for any other clever scientific reason, and it is entirely sensible that modern classes, such as the Soling, Tempest and 5.5 Metre should have eschewed them. They tend to increase the expense of racing, because they call for extra powerful winches, large strong crews, and the sails themselves are very difficult to make well. They have one virtue – they enable more sail to be set on the same spars. Of course they were originally intended as light air sails, at their best on reaches, but it wasn't long before they were being carried up hill and down, blow high and low. Modern offshore practice is to shift from a no. 1 genoa to no. 2 which merely means changing a sail of a light weight cloth for one of the same overall size made of heavier material. It has to blow above 18 knots before the average modern offshore yacht starts setting a smaller headsail than the maximum size genoa.

Mainsail sheeting

Mainsails were at one time always sheeted from the ends of their booms. This seemed to give the easiest control, for the mechanical advantage of the sheet was certainly enhanced by giving it a longer lever arm. But then sailors become conscious of mainsail twist – the tendency for the top of the sail to sag further to leeward than the bottom. Since the wind didn't twist in nearly the same way it became obvious that if a sail was twisted, some part of it must be at the wrong angle to the wind. Hard on the wind, with the boom end almost within the boat, most of this twist could be countered by simply pulling the sheet in very hard and letting the mainsheet traveller as far out as possible on the mainsheet track. But once the boat was headed further off the wind and the sheet had to be slackened, the twist suddenly increased.

Centre sheets

It wasn't difficult to see that if the sheet was brought further forward towards the centre of the boom, the angle at which twist could still be dealt with effectively by the sheet was greatly increased. For one thing the mainsheet track could be lengthened since the boat was wider amidships than at the stern and for another, the middle of the boom never swings out as much as the end of the boom. So mainsheets are now mostly to be found rigged ahead of the helmsman and sometimes almost in the middle of the boat. They need more purchase in this position, but they do a better job in countering twist.

Elvstrom-built Soling showing arched mainsheet track with mainsail sheeted very close to the centreline. The jib is similarly sheeted close to centreline, and on a track. Close sheeting will only work if the sailmaker has built twist into his sails and if the sheets are not hauled in too tightly. Note short traveller to permit main shrouds to be slid forward. Both crew are right over weather topside with only their feet showing.

François Richard

They also do something else – they permit the mainsail to be carried at wider angles when sailing on the wind in heavy weather. For it has been found that as wind increases and stability becomes vital, one way of keeping a boat on her feet is to let the mainsail further out so that it makes a smaller angle to the wind. In this way the sail is 'feathered' and speed through the water is increased. The boat cannot sail quite as high on the wind but she will probably get to the weather mark sooner because she is being kept more upright and therefore makes less leeway. She is also moving over the waves better and requires less weather helm.

Another advantage of the forward sheeting position is that it imposes load on the right part of the boom. As the sheet tension is increased the boom tends to bend downwards from the middle. This takes some of the belly out of the sail. With the sheet attached to the boom end all the strain comes on the leech, which becomes over tightened while the middle of the boom is allowed to bend upwards, throwing still more belly into the sail, which is exactly the reverse of what is needed.

Mind you, too much boom bend downwards is as harmful as anything other than an upward bend, for it allows the clew of the sail to move fractionally closer to the tack, which naturally increases the ability of the whole sail to fall in a bag to leeward. This is why stiff booms are the rule today, though some still flirt, unconvincingly, with bendy booms. But midships mainsheets are more and more popular as crews get to grips with the problem of ridding their mainsails of twist.

How far in or out to sheet your mainsail when on the wind will depend upon the class you are sailing in, crew weight, the weight of wind, the fullness of the sail and several other factors, by which I mean that you will simply have to experiment yourself. But we will deal with details of this sort when we consider tuning.

Headsail sheeting

For reasons I have already mentioned – the shape of the slot being most important – the correct sheeting of the headsail is critical. With overlapping genoa type jibs it is much more

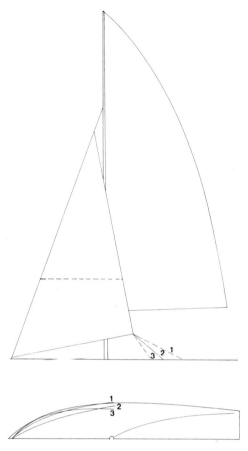

The fore and aft adjustment of the jib lead has a critical effect on the performance of the whole rig, since it vitally affects the slot shape. The effect on the section of the jib along the pecked line is shown in the lower drawing. If the lead is moved aft, the foot of the jib is tightened, the leech slackened and the slot widened. If the lead is moved forward the foot is slackened, the leech tightened and the slot constricted, while more flow is thrown into the jib.

The fore and aft position also affects closewindedness, because if the leech is loosened by moving the lead aft, the leech will fall off and it will not be possible to point as high. Conversely, if the lead is brought forward, the leech will be brought closer in to the centreline and the boat can point higher.

As a rough guide, position the lead so that leech and foot feel equally tight, but since the leech is longer than the foot it will have to be stretched more to register the same tension. In heavy weather, tend to move the lead aft to open up the slot, even at the expense of closewindedness. In light weather try moving the lead forward for maximum closewindedness. Raking the mast aft has the same effect as moving the jib lead aft.

important than the sheeting of the mainsail. It should not be difficult to grasp that the larger the size of headsail in proportion to mainsail, the more important, comparatively, the correct setting of the headsail becomes. In the case of modern ocean racers, the whole rig is designed around the need to set the headsail as well as possible. With the jib, the position of the fairlead must be considered in two dimensions – laterally and longitudinally. Each plane is as important as the other. A decade back, sailors hardly worried about lateral sheeting; they simply positioned the leads as far outboard as they could be fitted. Ted Hood designed an extra beamy 12 Metre *Nefertiti* just so that he could get his fairleads slightly further away from the centreline. This way he reasoned that he could make himself still bigger genoa jibs and have a still bigger overlap and slot without spoiling his mainsail. Wind tunnel tests conducted by the aeronautical department of Southampton University bore out this theory. Yet *Nefertiti* never got to defend the America's Cup for the USA, and since then tuners have been greedily learning how to get away with leads that are inching their way in towards the centrelines of the boat. They are doing this for one reason and one reason only – to point closer into the wind when beating. In recent years Dragons have moved their leads several inches inboard. The latest ocean racers sometimes lead sheets close to the coachroof coamings. In the case of classes with old fashioned narrow jibs without much overlap, such as the Star and Soling, jib leads are often less than 7 degrees to the centreline – and next year they may well be closer still.

Part of this move in offshore boats may be explained by the increased beam of these animals – the angle to the centreline may not actually be decreasing at all. Yet the fact remains that sailors are now very conscious of the need to experiment with the lateral positioning and they reason that if they can get their sails to set well with the lead an inch closer to the centreline, they should point a fraction higher.

It is not nearly as simple as that. In the faster, more powerful boats, particularly multihulls and trapeze classes, all experiments at moving the lead inboard have been very inconclusive and it is certain that boats, except sometimes in the smoothest of seas and the mildest of winds, do not point any higher for it.

In the classes where close sheeting has become the rule it is noticeable that a certain amount of induced twist in both mainsail and jib is essential, the twist of the jib matching the twist of the main so that the slot stays open from top to bottom.

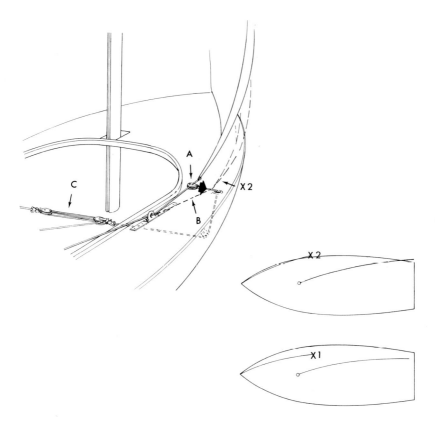

When reaching the jib lead needs to be taken as far out to the side as possible, and the device called a Barber hauler is useful here. The block (A) is clapped over the jib sheet and passed through a sheave or eye as far outboard as possible (on an offshore racing boat probably a fitting on the rail). Some boats might need a tackle (C) to haul the block out in the direction of the heavy arrow, giving the improved position (B). The drawing shows a Barber hauler adjusted for a fine reach, but a lot of skill can be shown in getting the attachment point and degree of outhaul exactly right for the conditions. The effect of the use of the hauler is shown, where the jib lead has been pulled out from X1 to X2.

It is not quite true that the angle of lead to the centreline determines the angle at which you can point. For one thing, the wind as it approaches the jib luff anticipates the object about to be placed in its path and alters course even before it gets there. How else can Flying Dutchmen profitably carry such fully cut, deeply bellied genoa jibs, the leesides of which appear to make a positive angle with the approaching wind?

The shorter, fatter, smaller and slower the boat, the wider the sheeting angle of the jib (and also the mainsail). Therefore dinghies will need wider sheeting angles than lean, classic yachts such as the Metre boats. The classes which can most profitably use narrow sheeting angles are those which need to be always feathering up into the wind, in order to hold themselves upright, relying on the inertial forces of heavy keels rather than the righting moment of crews on trapezes or with feet under hiking straps. This explains why the over-canvassed, heavy keeled Star goes so well with the jib sheeted almost on the centreline. It has to be pinched, not powered.

Once off the wind, it is commonly thought that jib leads can profitably be moved outboard. The best way of doing this is to fit Barber haulers – alternate, auxiliary leads which can pull the jib sheet out of its normal on-the-wind line. The rules of course prevent them being extended outboard. But you may well come to the conclusion, particularly in classes with spinnakers where there is much else to be done when off the wind, that these devices are not worth their weight and complexity.

Longitudinal sheet lead position affects the vital slot, even more than lateral lead. Luckily the rules and theory are pretty straightforward. If you move the lead further aft, you will tighten the foot of the jib and slacken the leech. This will effectively increase the width of the slot and help the flow to the lee side of the main. This is good news. The bad news that comes with it is that you will not be able to point as high because the leech of the jib and the top part of the sail will be twisting off to leeward.

If you move the lead forwards the reverse happens. The leech will tighten till the slot is so constricted the mainsail will probably begin to back unduly and your boat will feel constipated.

Detail of another Flying Dutchman showing underdeck jib fairlead with lateral as well as vertical adjustment. The theory is that in light weather the lead is set low and inboard, to tighten the leech and improve pointing. In heavier winds the lead will be raised and brought outboard to ease the leech, open up the slot, and enable the boat to foot fast rather than point high.

Two-dimensional jib sheet adjustment of an early type, seen aboard a British 5.5 Metre. Modern systems allow for quicker, under-sail adjustment. Snubbing winch has underdeck handle, the sheet being led to the cam cleats on the cockpit coaming.

If your jib has the traditional mitre seam running diagonally from clew towards the luff, begin by siting your fairlead about 10 degrees forward of the extension of this mitre to the deck. If, as is likely nowadays, your jib has no mitre seam, bisect the angle which the foot makes with the leech at the clew and continue this to the deck, then bring the fairlead about 5 degrees forward.

The jib leech, when sailing on the wind, should be tighter than the jib foot, partly because the leech is longer than the foot. But let your main guide be the backwinding of the luff of the main. If it is too pronounced the lead will have to come aft.

In fresh breezes the jib lead will need to be further aft than in light airs, for in fresh conditions the slot will need to be opened to help with stability, and by easing the jib leech the jib itself will contribute less to heeling. As with the need to increase the angle of the main boom to the centreline when hard pressed to windward, the point is that in heavy conditions it pays to keep moving fast through the water – footing – even if it is necessary to sail further off the wind in order to do so. The boat which tries to keep pointing high will inevitably sail so slowly that because of the waves and the wind, it will end up by making so much leeway that it will find itself further to leeward than the boat which began by pointing lower but moved through the water faster. I have never seen Paul Elvstrom win in a hard breeze by appearing to point higher than his rivals. He always gets ahead by powering through the lee of others.

The importance of the correct jib fairlead position, and also the need to move it for different wind strengths, is proportional to the size of jib. It is not tremendously critical with conventional dinghy rigs in which the jib does not overlap the mast and is less than a third of the area of the main. Experiments I have carefully made with an Enterprise which went fast

This standard Elvstrom-built Soling shows the self-tacking jib rig with the sheet track radiused about the jib tack and the wire sheet attached to the jib by a metal clewboard with optional attachment points for fine adjustment of leech/foot tension. Note how close to centreline the jib is being sheeted. Note also the spinnaker pole attachment fitting which slides up and down mast without needing a wind-catching track on the foreside of the mast.

François Richard

enough to win the National and East Coast Championships showed to my satisfaction that an inch or so of difference fore and aft made hardly any difference. Neither did lateral adjustment, though I did find it more harmful to position the lead too far inboard than too far outboard.

Jib height

In classes where tolerance in jib height is granted it does seem to pay to set the jib as close to the deck as possible. The Snipe class was the first, to my knowledge, in which this fact was exploited. If the jib foot is roughly parallel to the line of the foredeck this lowness will help still more. By closing the gap between jib and deck one can prevent air escaping from the higher pressure weather side to the lower pressure lee side and so spoiling the pressure differential. Closing the gap also helps the air to flow horizontally and irons out turbulence, as has been proved by the use of wool tuft telltales on the lower part of headsails on many different boats and wind tunnel models. In the Flying Dutchman class where the foresail itself is not measured (only the triangle formed by the jib halyard block, the jib tack and the jib fairlead) it is now common to cut a maximum size skirt to the jib foot (this skirt is now limited) so that the first jet of spray will wet the sail fabric and virtually seal the bottom of the sail to the foredeck. Lowering the jib also opens up the top of the slot – but it does hamper visibility and one should study class rules to see whether jib windows are allowed.

The Flying Dutchman class is specialized in another respect: because of the unusual method of measuring the headsail, jib fairleads are always fitted as far aft as possible and so it is not possible to move them further aft to ease things in a hard wind. But in this class, because of its large headsail, it has been found vital to ease the jib leech as wind increases. The solution to this problem was to arrange for the rake of the mast to be adjustable (rake is increased by slackening the jib halyard while taking up on shrouds). Increasing the rake will obviously ease the jib leech. This is an interesting example of how class rules and design peculiarities call for specialized techniques which may be of no value in other, apparently similar, classes.

66

Mast rake

It is becoming increasingly common practice in keel boats to allow the masthead to move forward (decrease rake) when going down wind. I held out against this policy when I first took to the Tempest class, for the simple reason that I could not see any logic in it. But experience has taught me otherwise. Downwind speed does seem to be helped if the masthead is moved forward. I now believe one gains by reducing helm needed to hold a straight course through waves. With the whole rig forward the boat wants to go straight more naturally and needs less speed-sapping correction. For this reason she will catch waves and surf more readily. In the Tempest I now do this by throwing off specially made shroud levers, once the weather mark is rounded. On offshore racers, hydraulic back-stay adjusters have been devised for the same purpose (though they are usually given only a few inches of adjustment). To counter the slop of a loose rig through waves, which can only be harmful, it is best to take up on the forestay or, in smaller classes, the jib halyard. The gain is less pronounced when reaching than on dead runs. I don't think it helps to any extent with centreboard craft for the simple reason that the centreboard is always swung aft in offwind conditions, which gives the same effect. This is why, coming from centreboarders, I at first scorned to bother about moving my Tempest mast.

Many believe that considerable aft rake is necessary for optimum windward performance. Manfred Curry conducted various experiments on wing shapes which always showed the greater efficiency of shapes incorporating a backswept leading edge. Yet he always seems to have ascribed the greater efficiency to other factors. He also said that the backswept effect of bird's wings did not improve flying speed so much as stability. But we would have to learn bird talk before we could check on the truth of this. Ice yachts, certainly the fastest sailing machines of all, have strongly sweptback masts but then they never use jibs. Supersonic aircraft carry very sweptback wings that are often completely delta shaped. But this is to lessen the buildup of speed of airflow over the wing leading edges, which should not be a big problem at our sailing speeds. It is difficult to find a scientific explanation of why masts need to be raked at least a

67

few degrees when hard on the wind but from experience I believe you will find that most experienced sailors recommend it. Note that we are talking of small racing craft with big mainsails. The offshore configuration of masthead genoa and minimal main is another matter. Here the first priority is the efficiency of the genoa which already has a sharply sweptback luff. I have heard it said that rake helps because it allows the

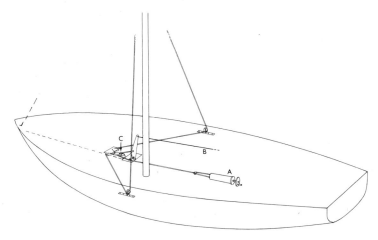

Speed can be increased off the wind if the mast is allowed to rake forward. Large boats can ease a standing backstay, and dinghies usually slacken their shrouds with a quick adjustment. For boats where price is no object this neat KWMS fitting instantaneously releases both shrouds by a controlled amount, which can be adjusted by the screw fitting (A). Normal operation is by the lever and line (B). It would be simple to modify this system by adding a block and then bringing the forestay back as shown in pecked line, round the additional block and attaching it to the moving block (C).

boom end to droop. When the outboard end becomes lower than the gooseneck, the sail finds itself with a second leading edge, and it has always been reckoned that the longer the leading edge the better. I don't find this argument convincing. Another theory has it that by raking the mast the centre of lift (area of maximum low pressure on the lee side) becomes more vertical because with an upright mast this line will obviously rake forward from the boom up to the headboard.

But don't worry too much about the reasons why. Most of the best skippers recommend some rake for the simple reason that they have found it pays off in winning races.

Leading edge

I have just touched on the question of length of leading edge. There is no doubt that aircraft experience here is born out in sailing. A tall, narrow sail will be more efficient, particularly upwind, than a short wide one of the same area. There is no doubt that sailmakers and sparmakers would find ways of making yachts' sailplans very much taller and narrower than they are today, were it not for the fact that measurement rules, such as the IOR, have begun to tax unduly high aspect ratios as it is believed that they may lead to mast failure and other undesirable things.

Again and again, owners faced with the need to reduce the ratings of their offshore racers have decided to lop off a considerable area of mainsail along the length of the leech, ending up with a smaller (because narrower) sail, but surprisingly as fast a yacht as before (at least when on the wind).

Flexible rig

We have already touched on the flexible rig question when we considered sail flattening as a result of mast bowing. Perhaps we should go into the problem in more detail now. Until the Thirties it was the determination of all crews to keep their rigs as stiff, upright and unbending as possible. There were a few yachts (such as the 6-Metre *Circe*) which always seemed to go best with some slack in the rig, but sailmakers would argue that if the spars were allowed to bend all over the place, how could they be expected to produce sails that set well?

Then along came the German Star sailor Walter Von Hutschler and his famous boat *Pimm*. In 1937 *Pimm* won four out of five races in the World Championships (she broke down in the fifth, and because the Star class insists that all races are counted for points, with no bonus for coming near the top,

Pimm did not win the title) and caused enormous interest, for her mast bent all over the place. *Pimm* won many other races with her bendy mast, and though her owner always insisted that the bend was only incidental and not the reason for her speed, keen skippers have been talking and thinking about bendy spars ever since. John Oakeley won the IYRU trials for a new two-man keelboat class with the prototype Tempest, using a Proctor alloy spar that was heavily bent, even in the lightest airs. Every Finn sailor bends his mast to a greater or lesser extent (but then, without rigging, he has no alternative).

Extremes do not pay

It seems to me that in yacht racing, extremes hardly ever pay. No sooner were the benefits of the bendy mast realised than masts were soon being allowed to bend far too much. The truth is that the best modern Stars bend their masts less than they were bending them fifteen years ago. All the best modern Tempests bend their masts less than Oakeley did with the first of the new class. On the other side, the best modern Dragons, whether they use the old wood or the new alloy spars, now use more bend than they used to when they only worried about keeping the pole as straight as possible. Even offshore skippers are playing about with bend (though I think they are misguided, as I shall explain later).

You may say that mast bend is here to stay, but the need for bend must be understood. So must the means of controlling it, for unless it is controlled and regulated it will surely do more harm than good.

The first efforts at bending masts were mechanical, by applying powerful screws at deck level. It was soon found that if the bend could be induced naturally, increasing as the wind increased and vice versa, there would be a gain in efficiency and a bonus in simplicity. One could never hope to operate screws quickly enough or promptly enough to match every wind variation. It was like trying to choose between three differently cut sails before a race when the very reason for having mast bend was to dispense with sail variation and hopefully evolve a single, universal suit of sails.

Absorbing shock

More recently, it has become generally understood that the object of mast bending is only partly to flatten sails so that the same area may be carried in higher wind speeds without ungovernable stability problems. Flexibility in the spar helps a boat get through a seaway and stay under control in puffy winds. Here we see the bend acting as a shock absorber between sail and hull, helping the sails to keep still even though the boat herself may be bouncing resoundingly from wave to wave. The kind of mast bend which will flatten an over-full sail must clearly be fore and aft roughly along the centreline. Bend which acts as a shock absorber and enables a boat to speed through waves more smoothly, and survive sharp, savage, jolting puffs with more equanimity, has to be sideways bend, for winds and waves strike the boat roughly sideways. If the mast is allowed to bend sideways too much, the boat will not point as high on the wind, but as has been explained earlier, there will come a time when the wind has increased to such an extent, and the wave height also, that pointing will matter rather less than speed through the water or 'footing' ability.

It may be stated, generally, that while some sideways bend,

This dinghy has a cam-type mast gate ram. For rough adjustment the cam is set in one of several slots in the gate; fine adjustment is by a line led aft to skipper. Such rams give excellent control of mast bend, but it is important that the gate holds the mast solidly athwartships (as here).

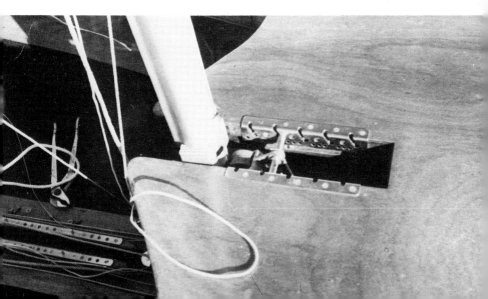

for boats that are destined to sail in open water and in breezy conditions is beneficial, one should be careful not to have more than is strictly necessary. Too much will be far more harmful than too little. Exactly how much will depend largely upon the type of boat and the comparative power one can bring to bear on the weather rail. Thus a heavier, fitter crew will go for a stiffer mast. One other aspect of sideways bend must be considered. As the top bends off to leeward, the middle of the mast will be encouraged to bow up to windward. The degree of this bend will depend upon the relationship of the length of the mast above the hounds to that below: the taller the topmast, relatively, the more influential it will be in making the middle of the mast bow to windward, while it bends to leeward. Many experts reckon that one should try to get the lower part of the mast to bend to windward in this way. They argue that it serves to open up the slot between mainsail and jib overlap. Certainly it seems to do this, but I have yet to see concrete evidence that any boat with a marked bend to windward in the lower portion of the mast was going better to windward because of it. The slot may be opened up but the set of both main and jib will inevitably be distorted to some extent.

Fore and aft bend, for mainsail flattening purposes, is a rather different matter. You would think that the shape of this bend should follow the curve cut into the luff of the mainsail. If this is done, most of the mast bend will be low down. In racing practice this has not been found completely desirable. It is less important to flatten the lower part of a mainsail than the upper part: the lower part, after all, will have much less heeling effect since it is acting only a few feet above the water. It is the top of the sail which is really trying to drag you over and slow you down. Therefore the mast bend should usually be more of a natural arc or bow with the maximum bend close to the half height.

A moment's consideration should reveal that the mast will naturally try to bend in this way. Consider the various forces:

Mast bend capability vividly demonstrated with an experimental Australian spar of stainless steel, a material which has yet to win wide acceptance. It enables a very small section to be used; fittings can be welded on but weight and stiffness are big problems. In fact, most good skippers will tell you that mast bend is best kept within very moderate limits – perhaps a maximum arch of 8 in. in a spar 23 ft overall.

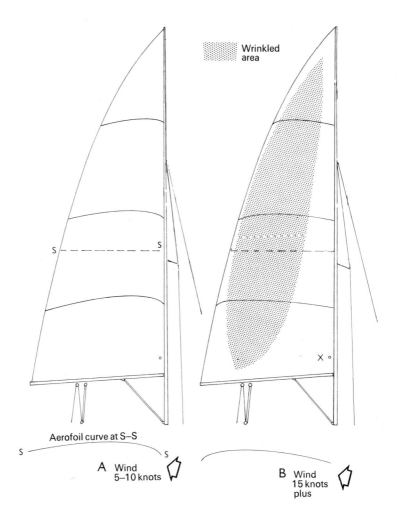

Wrinkled area

S —————————— S

Aerofoil curve at S–S

S ————————— S

A Wind 5–10 knots

B Wind 15 knots plus

there will be the considerable compression of the various shrouds and stays and halyards. Acting as they do up and down the mast these will attempt to buckle it to one side or the other. Then there is the tension of the mainsheet; whether this is at the outboard end of the boom or further forward it will serve to tighten the leech of the sail more than the luff. This tension will encourage the top of the mast to curve aft while its other effect will be to compress the boom towards the mast. Unless this effect is checked, the boom, pushing on its gooseneck, will

Mast bend and control of the sail section: the reason for bending masts and the sometimes complicated systems of applying and controlling bend is the need to preserve the best possible aerofoil section for the mainsail in varying wind conditions. A is a sail which, hoisted on a straight spar, assumes the medium fullness shown when the wind is 5–10 knots. When the wind exceeds 15 knots or so the sail, on a stiff spar, is likely to have assumed the shape in B, with maximum draft too far aft. The whole shaded area, where the battens are trying to do an impossible task, has become a mass of creases and puckers that destroy lift and increase drag. In C the Cunningham hole (X in drawing B) has been sweated down with a purchase and the mast, with an adjustable slot at the gate and suitable arrangement of mainsheet and kicking strap, is designed to bend. It goes slightly forward between the step and the hounds, helped by the forward pressure from the kicking strap transmitted through the boom. The transmitted spring from the masthead, which is pulled back by the mainsheet's pull working mainly along the leech of the sail, makes the whole spar assume a fair curve. The top of the mast may bend a little to leeward, causing the lower part to curve fractionally to weather – widening the slot, some people call it – but most of the curve is only in the fore and aft plane. The effect is a flatter but still well-shaped sail reasonably free from creases except round the Cunningham hole, where they do not matter much. You have in effect transformed your nicely arched light weather sail into a well-shaped hard weather one, and can reverse the process if the wind falls.

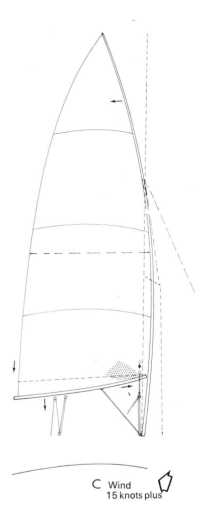

C Wind
15 knots plus

bend the lower part of the mast forward. The forestay will tend to pull the mast forward at the point where it meets the mast (commonly about two-thirds up). So there will be two forward forces, the boom acting low down and the forestay higher up, with a single backwards force acting on the top of the mast through the tightening of the leech by the mainsheet.

Without counter influences this will result in a bow that is too pronounced. If unchecked it will flatten the sail in quite light breezes when we would rather have a full sail and straight spar, and in a breeze it will try to over-flatten the sail, causing harmful distortion showing in pronounced creases from the boom end upwards, and a flapping leech.

So, in practice, with our modern, slim and lightweight spars, it is more a matter of keeping bend within bounds than of forcing a mast to bend in the first place. The means of controlling this bend will vary from class to class depending upon the design of the original rig and the latitude allowed by the class rules. Most One Design class rules do indeed allow some latitude in the design of the rig. To see the best way of controlling mast bend it is best to take a class such as the Flying Dutchman or 505 where the rules are most open and rig development consequently least inhibited.

Standing rigging

In both these classes it was once common to see all manner of different rig systems. Most people had diamond wires running over lateral spreaders to counter sideways bend and then fitted gadgets or blocks at deck level to control the amount the boom pushed the lower part of the mast forward.

Some classes with very tall masts and insufficient under-standing of bend and the harm done by windage, fitted multiple diamond wires and spreaders. The International 14 class was typical. I have seen an aged spruce 14 mast explode into pieces on an almost calm day, simply because it was no longer able to cope with the colossal compression forces resulting from all those tight wires.

Today, though, almost every leading Flying Dutchman and 505 relies on the same apparently simple and aerodynamically very clean method of staying: single shrouds run over single backswept spreaders joining the mast somewhere above the mid-point between deck and hounds.

Spreaders

Though this rig appears simple, the exact length and angle of spreaders and their method of attachment are vitally important in effecting bend. In the early days these spreaders were usually allowed to swing horizontally. It was reasoned that this would enable the lee shroud to swing clear of the lee side of the mainsail when the sheet was eased. It certainly did this, but it was gradually found that unlimited swing spreaders failed to control mast bend. As the mast bent more and more it also bent up to windward where the spreader met the mast, giving too much side bend and a slack forestay. So, as a cautious compromise the swing of the spreaders was limited to a few inches. This was better but it was not so good as entirely rigid, fixed spreaders, which could not swing at all (even though they did cut more into the lee side of the sail).

Having decided that fixed spreaders were best, there remained the two questions of length and backward angle. The natural angle would appear to be the same as that of the chainplate to the mast at deck level. If the angle is increased beyond this, more bend will be induced. If it is decreased (so that the spreaders sweep back less), the mast will appear to be stiffened. Spreader length affects bend too. If the spreader is so long that it forces the shroud out of line, bend will be increased. If the spreader is shortened until the shroud is actually pinched in and has to be held at the spreader end to prevent it jumping out, bend will be decreased.

If you think about this a bit, you should realise that by inhibiting bend, by angling the spreaders less and by cutting them shorter, it should be possible to use a smaller, lighter mast. This will obviously lead to a gain in stability and efficiency since the mainsail will have less turbulence from the smaller mast section. So, in classes such as the FD and 505 where different mast sections are permitted, very small masts are now carried successfully, using short, fixed, backswept spreaders which do all they can to keep the mast straight, the mast, in practice bending just the right amount for the flattening of the sail to match the crew weight and fullness of sail cut.

Proctor Metal Masts now have a very neat·spreader attachment fitting which permits the spreader angle to be screw adjusted, while the spreader length is adjustable too. I suggest you start with an angle that matches that made by the chainplate and mast at the deck. On the average size dinghy, fix the spreader length to distort the shroud outwards by about $1\frac{1}{2}$

inches. If the mast now bends too much, shorten the spreaders $\frac{1}{2}$ inch at a time. If the mast tends to bow up to windward too much at mid-height, decrease the spreader angle about 3 degrees at a time. If the mast appears to sag in the middle and flatten the main insufficiently, first of all increase the backswept angle of the spreaders, and if still insufficient, increase spreader length slightly. You will be surprised how much small adjustments of $\frac{1}{2}$ inch of length or 3 degrees of sweep can affect mast bend. Of course this sort of fine adjustment will not be easily possible without a spreader attachment such as the Proctor type.

As I have said, I am quite satisfied that the fixed backswept spreader is the best method of supporting the modern dinghy and small boat spar. Latest thinking, pioneered by David Hunt, is towards raising the height of the spreaders to about two-thirds distance up from the deck to the hounds. The reasoning for this is that since the mast is held firm at keel and deck it is cantilevered, and hence the lower part needs little support. Most modern arrangements allow the mast to move fore and aft at deck level, to a controlled extent without being able to move significantly sideways).

The older type of diamond wire over short, straight spreaders is good for controlling sideways bend and also serves to limit fore and aft bend, but used with a very limber mast the torsional strains on the spreaders will be very great, while however efficient the diamond rig may be, it will always need two extra wires compared to the backswept rig, which relies only on the shrouds.

The problem of the masthead rig, as used on almost every ocean racer, is quite different. In recent seasons keener skippers have been attempting to bend their masts to flatten their mainsails. They have to do this by brute strength since the masthead forestay completely counters the bending effect of the mainsheet tightening the leech. The accepted method is to fit a single, lower forestay. This is made extremely tight and helps to bow the mast forward at mid-length.

But to my thinking, such bending experiments are no more helpful than the cult of boom bending which visited our offshore racers a season or so after *Intrepid* won the America's Cup with a bendy boom. I feel she would probably have won

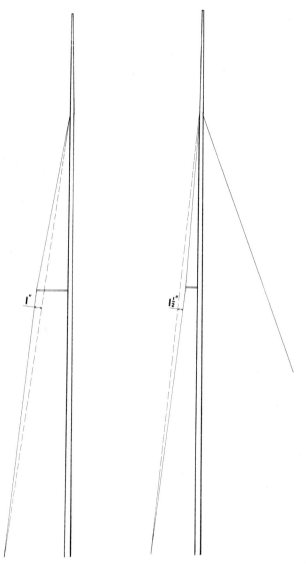

1" 1½"

If a modern, minimum-weight dinghy mast is not to bend unduly, the best rigging method is to fit backswept spreaders so arranged that the shroud is deflected forward about 1½ in. from the straight line. While helping to reduce fore and aft bend this will still allow the 8 in. or so now deemed correct for boats of around 16 ft. Seen from ahead, the spreaders should be of such a length that the shroud is deflected outwards about 1 in. If the mast is held at both keel and deck, it is best to fit the spreaders at two-thirds of the distance from the deck to the forestay attachment point.

still more easily without that boom. I feel that no ocean racer went any faster with a bendy boom, and they have all but vanished from the scene today. Neither do I believe that any modern ocean racer goes any faster because of bending her mast.

In a masthead rig the important sail, to which all rig tuning should be directed, is the genoa jib. To set this best a tight forestay is needed and the best way of maintaining a tight forestay is to keep a straight mast. As soon as the mast is bent the mast height is reduced and the forestay eased. Besides which, the mainsail on the modern ocean racer is so tall, narrow and small, and has to work behind such a thick mast (needed to support the forestay), that it is only minimally efficient anyway. Stability will be increased hardly at all by attempting to flatten the main.

Much better, instead is to try to reduce the sectional size of the mast (far too few masthead rigged masts are sufficiently tapered at top or bottom). Backswept spreaders are unnecessary on masthead rigged yachts because these normally fit permanent backstays, which are the best way of supporting the mast and preventing it from moving or bending forwards. Spreader lengths should be governed by genoa sheeting requirements – if they are too long, or fitted too low, it will not be possible to harden in the genoa sheet sufficiently for windward work. A reduction in spreader length for this reason may well call for the fitting of a second set of spreaders and so have a two-panel instead of a one-panel rig. It is interesting to note that though two-panel rigs are still in a small minority among offshore racers of under One Ton size, that the current holders of the One Ton and Half Ton Cups both sport two-panel mast rigs.

Bending booms

Be wary of bendy booms because for adequate strength they will need to be heavier than comparable stiff booms. Secondly, if the bend is exaggerated the distance between mainsail tack and clew is actually reduced, so that the whole sail will actually end up fuller, even though some of the belly is being pulled out by the downwards bend of the boom. As I have explained already, belly in the bottom of the sail is doing little harm as it contributes so little to heel.

4   The Race – First Thoughts

If it is possible to level a single generalized criticism at racing sailors it is that they tend to set too much store by their boats and too little by their own ability as competitors in the race. And since we have been considering the qualities of the boats at considerable length, it is high time we restore a proper sense of proportion by thinking about the race.

One has to admit that there are specialized classes, usually the exceptionally fast boats such as the FD and various catamarans, where the pure speed of the boat can occasionally make more difference than the sailing ability of her crew. Yet the great majority of the readers of this book will be racing smaller, slower, simpler boats than the FD, belonging to classes in which modification and refinement is pretty rigorously proscribed. They will have to depend more on themselves and less on their boats. When it comes to handicap racing, whether in dinghies or under the IOR or other offshore rating rules, boat speed in its pure, restricted sense will still mean less than a low rating (or good handicap), while handling and racing ability will more than often make the vital difference.

The boat, as we said at the very beginning, is only the weapon. Surely the hand in which it is held matters more.

If races were conducted in wind tunnels in which wind direction and speed could be completely depended upon and water currents entirely neglected, racing tactics would become matter of course and boat speed would soon become all-important. Thankfully, we do not race in wind tunnels. We race out in the open and to a very large extent are at the mercy of the elements. No matter where you are, whether in the lee of a towering grain elevator, at the head of a narrow river, or in mid-Atlantic thousands of miles from anything that might appear to hinder the consistency of the wind, you will find that it is constantly variable both in strength and direction. There is no such thing as a steady breeze. It is never steadier than 'comparatively steady' and it is usually extremely wilful and unreliable.

Grab your opportunity

This basic fact should condition our whole attitude to racing. Instead of being a straightforward, rule of thumb business it is a matter of responding to changing circumstances. In a word, it is above all an *Opportunist* sport. This of course is half its fascination. No crew, however badly placed, is completely without hope or completely beaten. No crew, however large their lead, is completely safe until the finish line is crossed. Often extra large leads constitute dangers in themselves.

What conclusions should be drawn from this? That when leading you should never relax and when being led you should never give up hope and that all the time, from before the start to the finish, you should try to 'stay loose' – by which I mean that you should be ready, on the instant, to abandon previous ideas about how that particular race should be conducted and opt for new plans. Only rarely does ground strategy outweigh field tactics in importance. One might have the most definite ideas about how to make a start and then, within a minute of the final gun, discover that a wind change has completely altered the premise upon which all your previous planning has been based. In the seconds remaining you must abandon your old ways and react anew.

Don't change horses

There will be many times when a change of plan would be a mistake because you are firmly committed to a certain line of action – it is then no good trying to change horses in midstream. Doesn't Macbeth point out in a nightmarish passage that once one gets into something too far it is as wearisome to go back as to go forward and see it through?

Tactics

Tactics are the essence of racing and they are as varied as the wind itself. Those who profess to find light air racing boring must be blind to tactical nuance. I started over an Olympic course in a wind so light that the race was stopped after four (instead of seven or more) legs. At times it was necessary to dip a finger over the side to make sure that we were making headway at all. We could not have averaged more than 2 knots, considerably slower than walking, yet it was not possible to relax for hours. There were major wind changes on each leg and race placings fluctuated just as widely. One boat which had rounded the first mark on the last of a breeze, against a current that held all others back from it for the next half hour, was soon to watch, becalmed and helpless, while the whole fleet brought up a new air towards him. We had as much fun that day as in any near gale and were given the opportunity of applying far more tactical resources. The total calm is exceedingly rare and the modern sailing craft will respond to airs so light that only cigarette smoke will detect them at all.

There are two sides to every race. First, you obviously have to get your own boat along as quickly as possible. To do this it must be well prepared and well handled. Second, you must take a better course than your opponents and this will not be straightforward. The fastest course and the straightest line between A and B hardly ever coincide in yacht racing.

Choosing your line

Unless the race is extremely short, it is unlikely that anybody will sail a perfect course from start to finish. Uffa Fox liked to say that if you only made one mistake you would be first, if you made two you would be second and so on. But obviously it isn't quite as simple as that. If there are more competitors the chances that the course will be correctly sailed by someone is statistically increased. So it is, if the competitors are of a high standard – as in Olympic competition. The chance of the course being correctly sailed is decreased if the race is very long or the fleet reduced in numbers. This obvious fact must have a considerable bearing on your own approach to a specific race. In a small fleet one can shape one's tactics more boldly, be more ready to go to extremes, to go all the way to one side on the windward leg, for instance. But if one is up against hundreds of others, one must be less concerned about sailing the perfect race for oneself, more concerned with sailing a better race than all the others, and this will usually call for fairly conservative tactics.

Series racing

When considering races with large fleets one is usually talking about a single race in a multi-race series, with the winner emerging as the one having the best score after say six separate races. Clearly, if one is seeking success in a series such as this, individual race success must be subordinated to the need for consistency over the full period. This again will inevitably mean tighter, more conservative tactics plus, towards the end of the series, a watchful policy of covering one's nearest rivals.

Scoring systems

Few skippers think about the major effect that different scoring systems have on race tactics though I am sure that the winners think more about this than the losers. There are still many race series where one only gets a single point for each boat beaten with no bonus for finishing high up, and where no discard is allowed. In such a system the winner is·more often than not someone who has not won a single race. He wins because of his sustained high level.

It should be seen that such an arrangement can lead to dullness for nobody is willing to take risks and everybody will, while watching each other, usually sail up the middle of the course. In recognition of this, and in recognition of the fact that luck – and bad luck – play a part in racing, it is now usual for skippers to be allowed to discard their worst placing in a series and to total the remainder. To the same end it is now usual for the points margin between first and second to be considerably larger than, for instance, that between twentieth and twenty-first.

How steeply the leaders should be aided in this way is a matter of hot debate. An earlier Olympic logarithmic scoring system gave such a big bonus to the winner that champions often emerged with two races of a series still left to be run. People began to feel that this favoured the gambler over the middle of the road man too emphatically; that luck was allowed to play too large a part. So the present Olympic system was introduced as a compromise (how often do we hear that word in sailing?) between the simple, straightforward, point-for-each-boat-beaten system which can lead to dullness, and the logarithmic system which strongly helps the leaders and is said to reward dangerous gambling and sheer luck. This current Olympic system has been adopted by a large majority of classes in all types of sailing and may well become universal, so I will detail it here since it does have a real influence on tactics.

It is a negative system, by which I mean that the winner scores the least. The winner always receives 0, the second 3 points, the third 5·7 points, the fourth 8 points, the fifth 10 points, the sixth 11·7 points, with seventh and all later places scoring their own placing plus 6. Mathematicians will see that this is a not completely elegant way of representing the curved line idea, boosting the race leaders, as the curve only starts at sixth place no matter how many are racing. Perhaps its greatest virtue is that it is easy and quick to calculate so that it is possible for competitors approaching the end of a series to see how they must place relative to their nearest rivals if they are to win.

Arthur Knapp, one of the US's hottest skippers, says, '*Be consistent, and don't get out on a limb.*' He in turn quotes an older American racing ace, Commodore 'Harry' Maxwell, as saying that the chap who wins is not the one who makes the smartest moves but the one who makes the fewest mistakes.

Now by nature I am against compromise and consistency and hedging one's bets and not taking risks – it is all so dull and dispiriting. I used to glory in pulling off dashing port tack starts, across the noses of the more pedestrian and conventional starboard tackers. I used to like to hurtle off to the lay line of what I had previously reckoned was going to be the paying side of the fleet.

But I didn't win as many races in those days as I now do by sailing more like a banker and less like a gambler. Again and again one hears people complaining about bad luck which descended upon them during a race in shifty winds. But why is it that the same people usually come to the top in these conditions, day after day? Are they simply luckier? I think not. They are more consistent because they sail a cannier race, laying themselves less open to the workings of fate, going less often to extremes.

Most people have an unconscious 'death or glory' urge which must be consciously kept in check. Most of us would rather come last one day if it meant that we might win the next day. So we allow ourselves to take very great risks which sooner or later are bound to pay off. Then when we come last we claim that Lady Luck struck us a foul blow below the belt and if we win we come in smiling in that easy way which indicates that we are used to the feeling. But it truly takes more strength of character to analyse the tactical risks coolly and objectively, react to them realistically and form one's tactics logically. Even if the result is a series of third and fourth placings without a single glorious victory, the chances of winning overall will be greatly improved. You might call this approach 'professional- ism'. It is more than ever essential in today's hot competition.

5   The Wind

Before we proceed to specific racing tactics and the particular parts of a race (which like chess should have an opening, a middle and an end game), let us consider the wind, the invisible element with which we are working.

Effect of height

Since water offers less friction to the passing wind than land, the wind tends to blow harder over water, and with less turbulence. There is also a tendency for the wind to rise as it flows. Tests have shown that it rises at about 4 degrees above the horizontal (though this varies just as direction and velocity vary). Thirdly, the wind aloft tends to move faster than the wind alow, because of surface friction offered by land and to a lesser extent by water, and also the inhibiting effect of the boat itself as it meets the wind. Wind which blows at about 8 knots nine feet above the sea may very well have speeded up to around 11 knots at 20 feet or towards the top of the average small boat rig. This speed gain will obviously make for a broader apparent wind. The apparent wind is very important in sailing: it is relative in speed and direction to the boat as she moves forward, and because of the boat's speed will always be from more nearly ahead than the true wind. Thus if a steam train travels at 60 mph with a true wind blowing from behind at only 30 mph, its apparent wind will come from dead ahead at a velocity of 30 mph. You always get a freer apparent wind near the top of the mast than lower down – a fact which lessens the urgency with which you should try to remove the last degree of twist from your sails.

Wind changes

There is a tendency for wind, in the northern hemisphere, to react to the pull of the sun and to follow the sun's course in a gradual veer through the day. (Wind is said to 'veer' when it shifts clockwise with the sun: if it changes in the other direction, say from north towards west, it is said to 'back'. Many people use the word 'veer' inaccurately to describe any change of direction.) This veering tendency is more marked in the afternoon and early evening than during the morning, when its effect is hardly discernible. In places of unusually steady winds, such as the Californian coast where placid weather and hot sunlight induce the same onshore breezes daily, the veer is so reliable that it is normal for knowing skippers to tack towards the right at the outset of every windward leg and only tack to the left when they come close to the right hand lay line. The veer is likely to be most marked in sunny weather.

The prevailing breeze for the south and west of Britain is the sou'wester off the Atlantic, born towards us by depressions. This wind is often associated with rain and is moisture laden and hence 'heavy' in the sense that it heels a boat considerably. It is subject to considerable shifts. On the south coast, because of the pull of the land this sou'wester usually has a lot of south in it, especially in sunny weather. Clouds coming up with the wind usually bring heavier flaws.

A less common wind is the easterly, which is usually very much lighter, more consistent and brings clearer weather. The summer of 1971 was notable for the large number of easterlies and was consequently a lighter season than usual, particularly at the beginning. The good old sou'westers reasserted themselves later. Until the 1971 season I would not trust an easterly to blow for more than a day at a time.

Any kind of wind from whatever direction is going to be more turbulent inland than at sea.

Shoreline effect

Where a body of water adjoins land the wind always tends to traverse the brink between the two at as broad an angle as possible. Ideally it would like to flow from one to the other at right angles. Waves also 'refract' in this way, trying to roll up the beach at right angles to it. Wind refraction obviously offers countless tactical racing opportunities and is one reason why a

89

good tactical rule is to sail towards the nearest land rather than away from it, when tacking parallel to, or approaching a shore.

Land and sea breezes

An important phenomenon in racing is the daily sea breeze blowing onto the shore from the sea. A wind blows off the sea because the land, during the day, becomes warmer than the nearby sea (which takes far longer to heat and far longer to cool than the land). The warmer land heats the air above it which expands and rises and leaves behind a space into which nearby cooler air is sucked. The nearest cool air is the air above the sea and so the cycle which causes the sea breeze occurs. The hot air rising over land is a 'thermal'. Glider pilots search continuously for these thermals and know that they are most likely to find them above terrain that heats quickly, such as sand, fields of ripe corn but not ploughland, forest or marsh.

It should be obvious that the sea breeze will be strongest on days of hot sunlight, when the land is heated quickly. It will obviously be helped if the breeze is already blowing in roughly its direction – as with the sou'wester along the south coast of England. If the day dawns grey and the wind starts by blowing from off the land the sea breeze is much less likely to build up and overcome the offshore breeze. Even when it does blow well, it hardly ever makes itself felt before noon and quite often fails to appear in any force before 13.30. Now it so happens that most major racing regattas which are held in coastal areas adjoining beaches are started around the time the sea breeze may be expected to start. So there is always the agonizing question of whether to tack out to sea in the expectation of more breeze, or to tack inshore in the hope of gaining through the previously described wind refraction over the shore, or for less current, or for similar reasons.

In my experience it hardly ever pays to head off for a sea breeze that has not yet made itself felt. The bet is too 'iffy'. Only go to meet it if you can see for sure that it is coming to meet you. Furthermore, there is often a calm before a sea breeze builds up on a perfect summer day, so racing will not start until either the sea breeze sets fairly in, or some other wind is born.

90

In the evenings land is supposed to cool down quicker than the sea so a breeze off the land asserts itself. But this doesn't seem to happen in British waters nearly as frequently as the daytime sea breeze.

Obstacles

Wind reacts to obstacles in its path in a way which would be completely predictable to the aerodynamicist. If it is flowing off the sea towards a high cliff, it will first tend to anticipate the cliff by lifting upwards well before the cliff face is reached, so causing an area of near calm some way to seaward of the cliff. Nearer the cliff the wind will become turbulent, and if the face is steep and tall enough there will be significant reverse eddies built up to fill the space left by the lifting air. If the wind is flowing over islands of any height there is likely to be an area of strong reverse eddies on the lee side of the islands. I know of little islets in Sydney Harbour which have very marked eddies of this type so that it is hardly possible to find a spot around them where one can luff up, head to wind, to anchor or nose into the beach.

Sailing inland it is simple to see that obstacles such as tall houses and bulky warehouses to windward are going to blanket you from the wind. What is less obvious is that the wind is likely to accelerate sharply through the gaps between buildings and that even if one is to windward of the buildings they will affect the wind by causing it to lift and eddy. Anyone doubting this should try to sail past the Needles into Fresh-water Bay, in a Round the Island race, in the normal sou'west wind. Progress is often quite impossible, not only because the waves are rebounding off the steep beach but because the wind is acting in this curious manner because of the cliffs. You have probably already noticed how, when tacking up a narrow river, you can often point up as you approach the shore until you sail nearly parallel to it. This is because of the wind refraction.

Looking for wind

Wind flaws, or squalls, tend to fan out radially. If the wind is on the beam and the squall is ahead of you it will first of all head you off. As you begin to pass it and leave it on your beam, it will progressively free up. This fact isn't important in itself because it should always be possible for you to detect the approach of the squall by its effect on the water surface, in ripples and catspaws darting hither and thither.

One is always told to head for clouds in search of more wind. Unfortunately clouds not only speed along much faster than most racing craft but they are continually forming and reforming as they go. So chasing clouds may often seem like chasing shadows. There will be times when sailing long courses on the sea when the choice of a windward leg could be decided by the presence of a particularly dark cloud to one side of the course. In that case do not be too greedy and sail too far, through too many headers or lifts, towards it. As you head towards it and you feel the wind alter in direction and velocity, act promptly to cash in.

You must always be careful to distinguish between the wind shift, which will be of a purely temporary nature, and what I call the 'wind bend', which will be much more permanent since it will have been brought about by some topographical or other feature such as a headland or bay. Your tactics will be quite different when dealing with the one or the other. Thus once you realize that you have properly entered a wind shift, and the wind has headed, you should tack without delay before the wind shifts back again. When you sail into what can be accurately diagnosed as a 'wind bend' you should usually sail further and further into it, being headed more and more. In this way you will be able to take full advantage of it. If you had tacked when you first felt the header you would sail out of it again immediately. This wind bend phenomenon is of great importance in coastal and championship racing and often dominates racing at such popular British racing centres as Torbay, Weymouth Bay and Poole Bay.

Wind speed definitions

Finally, a keen sailor must be familiar with different definitions of wind speeds. When the Americans and British race on the continent of Europe they are inclined to be confused by the metres per second designation commonly used there. Conversly, our knots (nautical miles per hour) sometimes confuse the Europeans. Both use the same Beaufort scale, yet this scale, used in summer, is not calibrated finely enough to be of much value, while the famous 'signs' used to describe a given wind speed may well vary in appearance from place to place and from one kind of weather to another. Thus wind on a fine sunny day may look less strong than it actually is, while overcast cloud and general dullness may make it look worse than it actually is. Also remember that when standing on a lee shore the wind will appear worse than it really is. The same thing may be said of dinghy parks when the wind whistles through the rigging of parked boats and half-hoisted sails flog wildly. Once you get out on the water you will probably find conditions better than you expected. These matters are important as early weather impressions will influence your choice of sails and the setting up of your rig.

And though it is usually quite easy to detect a freshening wind, it is much more difficult to detect a moderating one. This fact is often of vital importance in offshore racing. The crew which first begins to increase sail, hoist a bigger spinnaker, and so on, will steal a decisive march. After being battered by high winds, probably still surrounded by big seas, tired and often in the dead of night, most people will refuse to let themselves believe that a wind is lightening and will say to themselves 'Let's wait and see'. But every storm has an ending and the problem is to detect the beginning of this end as soon as it arrives.

Most summer racing is conducted in the lower scales of wind velocity. In the average racing craft the wind is going to feel quite hard and sailing is going to be tough work from about 14 knots upwards. In fact the skipper of a Finn is going to have to sit out and generally exert as much muscular energy at 14 knots as at 30 knots. The only difference is that at 30 knots he will need more seamanship and will have less respite. Most small boat racing is cancelled before the wind reaches a steady 30 knots, though this will depend on the area. Usually such features as the ability of a committee boat to hold station at anchor or the availability of an adequate number of rescue launches will influence the decision on whether racing is to be

held or not, rather than the ability of the racing boats themselves to handle the conditions.

Remember that 1 knot is 1 nautical mile per hour. One
metre per second is very slightly less than 2 knots and is 2·24
m.p.h.

Beaufort force	Knots	Metres/sec.	Indicators
0 Calm	less than 1	1.7	Water not rippled
1 Light	1–3	1.7–3	Ripples, smoke drifts, flag stirs
2 Light breeze	4–6	3.1–4.7	Small waves, wind felt on face
3 Light to moderate	7–10	4.8–6.6	Scattered white-caps, light flag extended
4 Moderate	11–16	6.7–8.7	Frequent white-caps
5 Fresh	17–21	8.8–10.6	Some spray, darting wind streaks. Trees sway
6 Strong	22–27	10.7–12.8	Large waves, extensive whitecaps, walking impeded. 'Yachtsmen's gale'.
7 Moderate gale	28–33	12.9–15.3	Foam streaks, boughs broken
8 Fresh gale	34–40	15.4–18	No small boats out. Breathing difficult when facing wind.

6   Tide and Current

Yacht racing nearly always takes place on a 'moving carpet'. The water upon which the boats are racing is hardly ever stationary but is moving one way or the other under the tide-generating impulse of the moon, the wind or for some other reason. If the whole racing area was moving uniformly and the turning marks were allowed to drift on the surface (as has happened in some experimental racing held in waters too deep to anchor turning marks), the water movement could be forgotten since it would effect all competitors equally. The truth is that the water movement is never completely uniform. Some areas of the course will have more movement than others. The movement may actually change direction during the course of the race.

since there are these differences you can be sure that there are also opportunities to turn to your advantage.

Effect of water movement

We needn't worry ourselves here about the causes of this water movement. Even those who do worry about the whole matter of tides are still far from a complete answer. But we should try to distinguish between currents and tides. Perhaps the biggest difference is that tides are predictable, whereas currents hardly ever are. The currents that abound in tideless waters like the Baltic and the Mediterranean's relatively tideless bays, and also in tidal oceans like the Pacific, have an amazing capacity for reversing themselves completely overnight and for doubling their velocity in a few hours. Usually it is possible to explain, in quasi-scientific terms, their odd behaviour, but it is far more difficult to predict. The best thing one can do is to map out the existing currents as late as possible before the race.

One of the features of racing in the late 1960s and early '70s has been the growth in the number of support boats which aim to help the competitor, whether operated by a proper team coach, a commercial sponsor or simply by friends. Such helpers are beginning to realise that with a fast launch and a simple little gadget they can map out the currents on a given course and hand the data to the competitor a few minutes before the start. Of course the competitor himself can do this too, but it will take him a great deal more time, and tire him before the race.

The current mapping gadget is simple enough. It consists of a small, low float weighted with 3 feet of light line. It can even be a partly filled bottle. The float needs to be low so that it will be unaffected by wind and the weight is needed to hold it down, away from the wind, and to give some idea of drift below the surface (the length of line should correspond with the draft of the racing boat). One motors or sails up to a mark before the start, drops the gadget overboard, then watches as it drifts away, noting the direction of this drift on a compass and, as a refinement, timing its rate of movement with a stopwatch (if you time its speed be careful to see that it is not affected by turbulence from the mark or its mooring line). To make a thorough job of current mapping, one needs to repeat the performance at each mark of the course, then sketch a rough map and study it carefully. I expect to see current predictors carried by most keen racing yachts in non-tidal waters, in the near future.

By and large, in any tideless waters – the Baltic is a good example – you can expect a prevailing wind to set up a significant surface drift. Any wind which has blown for more than a day or two from the same direction is likely to set up such a drift. However, as Newton pointed out, what goes up must come down and after a certain drift has been going the same way for a day or two there is likely to be set up, a strong counter influence. Then if the wind should drop or alter, look out for a quick reversal of the current. And nearly always there will be local topographical features to impose their own special influence. At Kiel there is usually a wind-induced surface drift, but this is strongly influenced by water flowing out of (or sometimes into) Kiel Fjord. Heavy rains (and there is a lot of rain in Holstein) will cause more water to want to flow out of the Fjord and into the open sea. One danger here is to accept without question current data assembled by naval or commercial shipping authorities. They will be concerned with water flowing 6 feet or more below the surface, and often there will be a counter current at this depth, below your keel, which will have no influence on you whatsoever.

Luckily the currents in non-tidal waters are so very complex and hard to predict that they even baffle the locals, so one does not suffer unduly by being a stranger, and if you take the trouble to map out the prevailing currents as I have suggested you can actually steal a march on those locals who will be inclined to sit back thinking they know it all. I cannot imagine that even the most knowledgeable locals predicted the astonishing current changes during the Tempest World Championship at Marstrand, near Gothenberg, in Sweden in 1971, but there were one or two who warned beforehand that there would be changes of some kind.

Tidal streams

Tides should be much more predictable. One has simply to refer to published tables. But here too, remember that winds may delay a change of tide or cause one to run higher and stronger. When examining tidal tables pay just as much attention to tidal heights as to tidal times. Few small boat sailors realise the full significance of the continual change of strength of tidal streams. The height of high water in Portsmouth can vary between 16·4 feet and 11·8 feet within eight days. The variation in velocity of the tidal stream nearby will be in direct proportion to this change (i.e. it might be 4·1 knots one day and 2·95 knots eight days later). Since the tide varies from springs (the biggest range and fast running streams) to neaps (least range and slowest streams) every week, it is easy to see how one might go completely wrong by trying to apply the experience of one weekend to the next.

Few small boat racers take full advantage of the inexpensive Admiralty *Tidal Stream Atlases,* which cover most areas. Some popular racing centres such as the Solent and Long Island Sound will spawn their own special yachtsmen's racing aids, many of which can be extremely useful.

Having discovered the basic direction of a current or a tide it is necessary to develop an understanding of its likely behaviour. From Bernoulli's theory it is easy to see that a stream will accelerate when constricted. Thus where the River Deben narrows at its mouth the stream is strongest, and so is the Solent stream at its narrowest part, Hurst Castle. Apparently at variance with this rule is the fact that the stream will also be strongest where the depth is greatest, and weakest where it is shallowest. This probably has to do with friction of the water against the surface of the seabed.

Choose your line

In practice, if you wish to take advantage of a fair stream you will sail down the middle of the deepest water. If you hope to cheat a foul stream you will sail against it in the shallowest water you dare chance. You will also look out for favourable eddies or counter currents if you are heading against a foul stream. These are likely to occur in the places you would expect if you have been studying fluid flow over sails and hulls. Thus a counter current or eddy may be expected in any deep bay adjoining an open stretch of water. You may also expect a back eddy of this sort on the outside of a sharp bend in a river or channel. You can also expect an eddy where the depth suddenly changes because of a rock shelf or similarly abrupt feature. Where the land offers an abrupt obstruction to the unimpeded progress of the stream, you should look for the helpful eddy. Observation and experience are your best guides. You can see an eddy as it carries along bits of flotsam, and you can spot the line between a stream and an eddy by the line of trapped flotsam. The higher, stronger tides will carry the most debris.

In many racing areas, especially in Britain, tidal streams are so strong that they completely dominate tactics in all but the heaviest winds. Instead of looking for wind shifts you will be following the currents. This can result in just as enjoyable sport. The difficulty is that when you eventually race in some big regatta abroad, the chances are that the streams will be weak and therefore the wind shifts all-important, so without wind shift sailing practice at home, you will find yourself at a disadvantage.

Effect on waves

Currents and tidal streams have a big effect on waves. The roughest waves will occur when the wind is blowing against the current. This demonstrates the big frictional effect between wind and water. A weather-going current will cause the steepest, shortest waves, the ones most likely to break and tumble aboard. When the current flows with the wind the waves will be at their longest and most regular because the current will have teased out the waves into a firm pattern. One of the main difficulties for the British, racing abroad after becoming used to tidal waters, is in dealing with the much more haphazard and tumbling waves to be met with in tide-free waters. These waves appear to us to be larger than they should for the strength of wind and to lack form and coherence. A different technique is needed to get through them quickly; different sails may be needed too and a different rig. But more of this when we consider tuning.

One phenomenon which is often experienced in river and estuary sailing is the extra drag which occurs when sailing in water which is only slightly deeper than the depth of the hull. Going to windward the need for lateral area and at least some centreboard will prevent this from ever happening, but it is quite common to be running downwind in waters so shallow that the boat begins to drag up a much larger than normal stern wave, which will make more noise than normal. This extra wave-making, caused by the normal stern wave impinging on the sea bed, will effectively slow you down. Hence, if cheating a tide, be wary of going into very shallow water where you may lose more from wave-making drag than you can expect to gain from an eddy.

Waves and racing

A few more thoughts about waves: obviously their size will

depend on the fetch, distance of unimpeded build-up and the strength of the wind. Waves respond almost immediately to wind changes, though a confused swell can run for days after a change. In the Mediterranean I have seen a sea build up well ahead of a wind increase. Waves near shore will always be smaller than those further out except in the case of breakers in shoaling water, and this is true of a lee or weather shore.

Guard against the specially confused back sea which will prevail off a deep and rocky lee shore or off a breakwater or other man-made obstruction. One can see wicked seas of this sort off Dover's extensive outer breakwater. Waves create an entirely new set of racing opportunities which can make more difference between who wins and loses than sail brand names, mast makes and that sort of thing. A helmsman who is adept at surfing can gain yards in a single leg over those who fail to make the most of their opportunities. A man who is clever at picking his way through waves upwind can sometimes gain almost as much. Most racing sailors in Britain have insufficient opportunity of getting open water practice and often lose out against Baltic, Caribbean and Australian rivals as a result.

7   The Racing Rules

After our unreliable power source, the wind and our moving arena, the water, there is a third parameter circumscribing our freedom of action in any yacht race – the Racing Rules. So I regret that it will be necessary to give some consideration to them before we can proceed to the racing itself.

Regrets are necessary, for rules in themselves are attractive to very few, while the yacht racing rules, whose latest version is the 1973 edition published by the International Yacht Racing Union, are prolix, inelegantly written and anything but a homogeneous entity.

The trouble is that everyone likes to dabble at the rules. Every delegate to the IYRU reckons he can make them just a little bit better. Each represents a country which has some particular grouse about a particular aspect of the current rules. The consequence is that the Rules Committee of the IYRU is absurdly over-large, and a consequence of this is that they can never leave well alone. The rules have hardly been revised, republished and fully understood by the world's harassed racing yachtsmen than another, newer edition is handed down to contain minor but none the less important revisions.

The plan now is to limit revisions to once in four years, the revisions to appear immediately after each Olympic Games (the next edition will be promulgated in 1977). But is it really necessary that the rules should be allowed to develop or 'progress' in this way? In the search for improvement only complexity seems to be achieved; the cause of simplification is hardly ever served, and the fact that the Racing Rules Committee consists of people from at least eight different countries hardly serves the cause of good syntax (the official language is English).

The present rules run to some 150 pages, but of these only a small portion concern actual right of way rules during a race. The rest is concerned with such things as definitions, race committee procedure, protest procedure, sailing instructions, rules of universal application to all racing craft, and so on.

Study the rules

You should force yourself through the whole length and width of these rules (copies are obtainable from the Royal Yachting Association, the North American Yacht Racing Union and all other national authorities) but for strictly racing purposes you should concentrate on the Definitions and on the Right of Way rules 36–46 inclusive.

A working knowledge of the Definitions is essential for proper understanding of the later rules. One of the short-comings of the present rules is that there are likely to be situations in a race where conflicting rules may apply to the same incident. You may think that this matter will be sorted out by the fact that certain rules are called Fundamental Rules and which one would expect to have precedence over all others. Yet there is another species of rule – Section E, Rules of Exception and Special Application – which only fog the issue.

But remember the bare bones of the Fundamental Rules, which begin with the cornerstone of all attempted ordering of converging sailing craft. Rule 36 says, 'A port-tack yacht shall keep clear of a starboard-tack yacht'. From the Definitions you will learn that 'A yacht is on a tack except when she is tacking or gybing. A yacht is on the tack (starboard or port) corresponding to her windward side.'

From which tortured piece of English you should deduce that if the wind is blowing over your port or left hand side onto your sails which are set to starboard you are on the port tack and will have to give way to all craft on the opposite tack. It matters not whether they or you are closehauled, reaching or running, or under spinnaker.

> The experts take risks which do not always come off. In the 1972 Olympics at Kiel, Durward Knowles of the Bahamas (1964 Star Gold Medal) crossed Germany's Willy Kuhweide (1964 Finn Gold Medal) so closely on port tack, that he later withdrew from the race.
>
> *Jack Knight*

As you will discover later, the starboard tack is a valuable weapon, since it will decide which of two level boats on opposite tacks is actually ahead in the context of the race. In crowded fleets wise boats start on starboard tack, approach marks on starboard tack and probably cross the finishing line on starboard tack.

The second Fundamental Rule concerns boats on similar tacks, and like the rules themselves it grows in complexity.

Rule 37 has three separate provisions. Rule 37.1 says, 'A windward yacht shall keep clear of a leeward yacht'. The Definitions help clear up any doubt about which of two yachts would be windward and which leeward. Any sailor should know that the boat which casts the wind shadow on the other is the windward yacht.

Rule 37.2 says, 'A yacht clear astern shall keep clear of a yacht clear ahead'. Now this is infinitely more complicated because it gets us into the whole grey area (heavily mined at that) of overlaps, rounding marks, approaching obstructions, and that sort of thing.

We must refer to our Definitions once more, where we learn : 'A yacht is clear astern of another when her hull and equipment in normal position are abaft an imaginary line projected abeam from the aftermost point of the other's hull and equipment in normal position. The other yacht is clear ahead'.

Is that clear, one wonders? Note that the equipment in normal position will include a rudder blade, which in dinghies commonly extends at least a foot further aft than the hull itself. Note also that the line is drawn at right angles to the rearmost position of the leading boat. It is not a line drawn at right angles to the bow of the boat behind (though it used to be). The consequence of this is that, as the leading boat begins to round up to turn a mark and its direction alters, the right angle line drawn from its stern will tend to open up and embrace boats coming up behind and hoping to grab an overlap at the mark (which is why the overlap limitations are clearly drawn). The real point of this rule is to require the overtaking boat, travelling faster, to keep clear of the boat being overtaken. Taken in conjunction with Rule 37.1 it may be seen that if the overtaking boat elects to pass the boat ahead on the windward side, she should be ready to keep out of the way if the boat ahead should decide to turn more closely into the wind, for the windward yacht (which the overtaking yacht will be) must always keep clear of the leeward yacht.

Rule 37.3 adds a further provision governing boats on the same tack: 'A yacht which establishes an overlap to leeward from clear astern shall allow the windward yacht ample room and opportunity to keep clear, and during the existence of that overlap the leeward yacht shall not sail above her proper course.' This simply spells out what I have already touched

It is nearly always best, when on port tack, to bear away under a right-of-way boat's stern as B is doing. With a slight easing of sheets as you do so, hardening in again the moment you are on the wind, you gain extra speed to make up for the few feet you have given away.

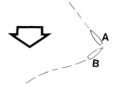

A2

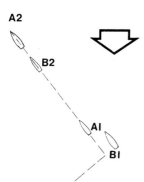

If you tack and lee-bow, as A is doing, you have no freedom of manoeuvre until you have sailed on enough to shake off B and weather him, and this loss of freedom to tack can be serious when other boats are threatening.

upon and plugs the gap left after grasping the combined intentions of Rules 37.1 and 37.2. It means that if you decided to overtake to leeward of the leading yacht, you must allow the leading yacht plenty of room to keep clear of you and you must not point up as if to collide. You will know that as sailing boats turn their sterns swing outwards, and take up quite a lot of room.

Note that phrase 'proper course' – it is always cropping up in yacht racing incidents. Summoning the Definitions to our rescue, we learn that 'proper course' is 'any course which a yacht might sail after the starting signal, in the absence of the other yacht or yachts affected, to finish as quickly as possible. . . . There is no proper course before the starting signal'.

Rule 38 deals with one of yacht racing's most cherished and honoured traditions – the freedom of a yacht to round up more closely into the wind, or luff. It may be seen that if (under Rule 37.1) a windward yacht must keep clear of a leeward yacht, and if an overtaking yacht must keep clear of an overtaken yacht (Rule 37.2), and if on top of all this a yacht shall be allowed to head up into the wind or luff, any yacht which elects to overtake another to windward should be alert for danger and obstructionism.

The rule is headed: '38 – Right-of-Way Yacht Luffing after Starting'. The distinction about 'after starting' is important since, as part 1 of this rule makes clear, a yacht may not luff as she pleases before starting. So Rule 38.1 declares that a yacht clear ahead or a leeward yacht may 'luff as she pleases' (hence without warning and as suddenly and as precipitously as one may), except that (and this exception is most important) she may not luff above her proper course while a special kind of overlap exists. The rule goes on to define this special overlap, which really only means that a windward yacht which overlaps the leeward one which wishes to luff, has now drawn so far up on the leeward luffing yacht that she is as good as past. The definition of this special overlap is 'about face' since it is described from the position of the helmsman of the windward yacht, whereas it is the leeward yacht which is having to act positively, luffing or not luffing as the case may be. When the helmsman of the windward yacht, from his normal steering position, finds himself either abreast or ahead of the mast of the leeward yacht the leeward yacht may no longer luff him and is forced to return to her 'proper course'. To signify that this point has been reached the helmsman of the windward yacht calls out 'Mast abeam' or sometimes 'Mast line'.

In other words, you may luff another yacht as hard as you like until that other yacht begins to draw past you. Then you must fall back onto your old course. Rule 38.2 describes the overlap business more fully, pointing out that overlaps only exist between yachts which are within two lengths of one another.

Rule 38.3 establishes the onus of luffing, stating that a leeward yacht's helmsman may luff until the helmsman of the weather yacht has hailed 'Mast abeam' or similar. The leeward yacht must then desist and if her skipper should consider the claim of the other to be wrong, he may only protest (of which more later).

Rule 38.4 points out that a windward yacht may not get so close to a leeward yacht that the latter is unable to luff her any more, unless the windward yacht is hindered in her free movement by a third yacht or an obstruction of some kind.

Rule 38.5 says that a yacht shall only luff other yachts if she has the right to luff all the yachts affected by her luff. If she has the right to luff all the others (because they are far enough back

Luffing: when being overtaken to weather a boat may luff as suddenly as she likes, and as far as head to wind. The luffer is allowed to hit the overtaker. But when the *overtaking* boat (B) has got so far that the helmsman in his normal position is abeam of the mast of the *overtaken* boat, he can hail 'Mast abeam'. On this hail the overtaken boat may no longer luff and must bear away onto her proper course. The overtaken boat only regains her luffing rights when the overlap has been broken. Both boats in a luffing match lose against another boat that does not get involved; note the relative positions of boats A, B and L at (1) and (2).

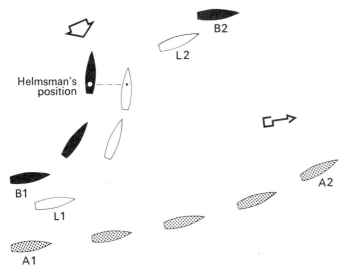

on her) they must all respond even though one may not otherwise have the right to luff another.

Luffing is an odd survival in yacht racing but a cherished one. It stems from the natural feeling of annoyance that anybody should have the temerity to come up from behind you and dare to sit on your wind, something that is very easily done when running before the wind with puffs tending to originate from astern. Translated into action, the annoyance becomes a luff. The reasoning for it is that anybody coming onto your wind does so at his peril. Note that before starting, when there is no 'proper course', one can only luff gradually and no closer to the wind than closehauled, giving another yacht every

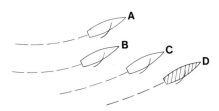

Luffing: boat D may luff A, B, and C and they must respond, although B on her own is not entitled to luff A.

opportunity of keeping clear. This right is given under Rule 37.1: 'A windward yacht shall keep clear of a leeward yacht.'

Rule 39 makes it clear that though a yacht may luff or head more closely up into the wind she may not turn the other way and head further away from the wind, which she might do in order to hamper another yacht which may be endeavouring to overtake her to leeward. A yacht may only bear away below her proper course when she is three boat lengths or more away from another to leeward, or clear astern but steering to pass to leeward.

Rule 40, which is really supernumerary, spells out (in the considerable length of 150 words) the point about luffing before starting. The right-of-way yacht must not luff closer than closehauled; after starting she may luff head to wind as she thinks fit.

108

One practical point about luffing: it usually slows the boat doing the luffing as much as the boat being luffed. So while it is fine in a two-boat match race and may be very valuable as a delaying tactic in a team race, it is hardly ever worthwhile in a big fleet where one has to beat not just the boat behind or to windward, but the entire fleet.

Rule 41 has a special section to itself but is not very important for all that. It makes it quite clear that a boat which is in the act of either tacking or gybing must keep clear of boats which are already on one tack or the other. By the definition of the Rules, boats are on starboard tack, on port tack, or tacking

Rounding marks: Rule 42 makes quite clear that a boat running or reaching on port tack can claim an overlap on another, on starboard. But before the leading yacht is within two of her overall lengths of the mark Fundamental Rule 36 applies and the port tack boat must yield right of way.

or gybing from one tack to the other. If two yachts are converging on opposite tacks and the port tack boat decides to gybe to keep clear of the starboard right-of-way boat, it must gybe soon enough so that its swinging boom does not incommode the right-of-way boat. Once safely gybed the old port tacker is now a starboard tacker and to windward, so must still keep clear under Rule 37.1.

In the unlikely event of two boats tacking or gybing simultaneously, the one on the other's port side shall keep clear. I have quoted verbatim since the provision is worded in such an Alice in Wonderland way.

Rule 42 starts off the special section E devoted to Rules of Exception and Special Application (how fundamental are your Fundamental Rules now?). This section is very important since it deals with yachts engaged in rounding marks, approaching obstructions to sea room, and that sort of thing, and it should be obvious that it is around marks and when heading for the shore, or other boats or rocks, that one needs to know one's rights under these rules.

Rule 42 is the longest and most complicated in the book, running to three sub-sections, each of which have up to five sub-sub-sections, in three of which sub-sub-sections there are – you guessed it – sub-sub-sub-sections. Added up, all these provisions mean:

a. Provided you have established an inside overlap in good time, the leading boat must give you room to round a mark or obstruction to sea room, inside.

b. It doesn't matter which tack you are on or whether the boats approaching a mark are on different tacks, the inside boat, having established her overlap, is entitled to room.

c. The only exception to this is when boats on different tacks are beating up to a mark (but then overlaps will not often be in dispute).

d. To establish your overlap in time, you must be overlapping the leading boat by the time the latter's bow comes within two lengths of the mark. Often, when at speed, this is very difficult to judge. Here is one area in which the rules could truly be improved.

e. An outside yacht must give room to all boats inside her which have properly achieved overlaps. It naturally follows that if A has secured an overlap on B, which is overlapping C, which is overlapping D, the latter – D – may find herself having to give room to A and B as well as C, even though A and B may not have achieved overlaps on D.

f. Once the overlap is obtained, one secures room to tack or gybe round the mark, but the leading boat must be careful not to tack too close ahead of the boat behind – she is then subject to Rule 41.1, 'a yacht tacking shall keep clear of a yacht on a tack.'

110

g. If the leading yacht disputes that the yacht behind has achieved an overlap properly, the correct course is to yield the necessary room, then protest later.

h. There is a special but common case when boats are fanning in at one end of the starting line in order to start: 'a leeward yacht shall be under no obligation to give any windward yacht room to pass to leeward of a starting mark surrounded by navigable water' up until the starting gun. After the starting gun the situation changes: that same leeward yacht may not now head up higher than her closehauled course or above the first mark, if the first leg is not to windward. This rule was of vital importance during the 1970 America's Cup match.

i. One can normally substitute any obstruction to sea room, including the shore or another yacht racing, wherever I have used the words 'turning mark' above.

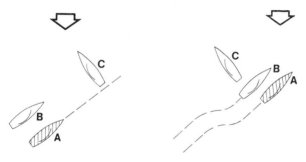

When the obstruction to sea room is another boat racing: even though A need not alter course himself to avoid the right-of-way boat, he must bear off to allow the overlapped boat to windward room to bear off under his stern if he elects to do this, instead of tacking (Rule 42.1 (a)).

While on the subject of marks, it is important to remember that a big change in the 1969 code enabled a yacht which touched a mark to continue racing. Before that date, a yacht touching any above water part of a turning mark was obliged to retire from the race. Under the new Rule 52 added for 1969, a yacht which touches a mark is now allowed the penalty of circling that mark before continuing. Note that as she circles the mark she has to keep out of the way of all other competitors regardless of whether she might be on the starboard right-of-way tack (a bad case of one rule contradicting another

111

– often a boat behind will not know that a yacht ahead is simply re-rounding to expunge a touching and will instinctively take avoiding action if on port tack). Note also that as a sop to the traditionalists, race officers are able to opt out of the new Rule 52 and continue to ask for the retirement of all mark touchers. But they must say so in the race programme.

The buoy re-rounding development signals a new trend in yacht racing – the desire to bring in lesser penalties than retirement for rule infringements. This trend receives official recognition in the 1973 code. A Race Committee is now allowed three options: (a) to insist that a fouling boat retire from the race, in the old way; (b) that the fouling yacht continues, but accepts a 20% place penalty; (c) that the fouling yacht exceutes a 720° (double circle) turn, as soon as possible after the foul, to expunge its foul. The initiative is left with the Race Committee and it seems likely that, in Britain, option (a) will continue to prevail.

To return to our stumbling progress through the thick underbrush of the rules, let us consider Rule 43. This deals with yachts tacking at, or standing into obstructions. You will understand that if two yachts are overlapped and headed for an obstruction such as the shore, the one nearer the obstruction may be unable to put in a tack to stand away from the approaching danger till the other has given him room to make his tack. In this case, the boat nearest the danger (which will be the leeward yacht) hails, calling 'Water', 'Room to tack please', or some such. The other yacht, normally the windward one must immediately respond by affording the other room to tack. Note that the boat hailed need not tack providing that she gives the other yacht room to tack. Note that the hailing yacht must tack very promptly after being given room and is not able to steal on for a few precious yards.

There is a special case here of somewhat rare application. If the approaching obstruction is a mark of the course which the boat hailed can weather but the hailing boat cannot, the boat hailed should return the hail by stating that he does not have to give room. If the yacht which first hailed cannot avoid hitting the mark in any other way but by getting the other to tack, the other shall tack but then the boat which first hailed must promptly retire. The only time you are likely to meet this case

112

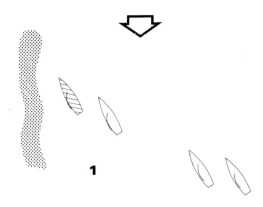

1

Calling for water: hail in good time when asking for water on approaching an
obstruction or shoal water. Once you have tacked onto port (2) your rights are
nil and you will face as here the threat of a series of starboard boats, or must,
with hardly any room, tack back again. When you have hailed you must go
about immediately when water has been given.

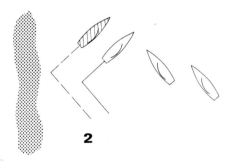

2

is when the turning mark is a lengthy moored vessel, or an
object like a detached mole.

Rule 43 comes into play most often when racing fleets are
close-tacking up a shore to avoid a foul tide. It happens again
and again in the Solent, especially during Cowes Week. Very
quick thinking is needed, and a certain amount of give and
take, if large yachts are not to get into very tight corners.
Often, one stands into the danger – in this case shoal water –
on the right-of-way starboard tack and has to come out, away

113

from the danger, on port tack. One can only hail for water when standing in. As soon as one has tacked and is on port one has to give right of way to all others on starboard tack still standing in. The safe rule here is to hail early and loud when on starboard, then try to look ahead and time one's tack in a way which will give you an avenue out on port tack, towards deeper water. But in handicap racing smaller, nippier craft will always enjoy an advantage in these situations over larger, potentially faster craft (which dare not sail as close into the shallows).

Rule 44 deals with a special case, the case of the premature starter who has been recalled and has to return to restart. Rule 44 makes clear that she forfeits all normal right-of-way rights and must avoid all proper starters no matter what tack she may be on, until she has returned to the right side of the line, when she again ranks fully. Note that under the most recent fashion for controlling very large starts, now so common, one is often instructed to return outside the limits marking the ends of the line.

Rule 45, oddly placed, makes it clear that boats involved in re-rounding a touched mark (Rule 52) must also yield all rights to others; not regaining them until the mark has been recircled and the race re-joined.

It does seem dangerous that there should be contradictions of this sort in the rules, arbitrarily taking away rights (such as those of the starboard tack boat) at certain stages in a race. Often, a boat behind, approaching a mark on port, will not realise that a starboard tacker is a re-circling mark toucher, so it will go out of its way to give the starboard tacker rights which she doesn't at that precise moment have.

The 1973 rules make it clear that if one touches a mark when in the act of finishing, one is not timed in until one has completely re-rounded the touched mark, even if one's bow may have already crossed the finishing line.

That is the corpus of the rules which are likely to be needed by the racing crew. There are of course others which impinge from time to time. Rule 31 talks about disqualification of a yacht breaking a rule. Rule 32 provides for the disqualification of a yacht, even if she has right of way, if she doesn't attempt to avoid a collision 'resulting in serious damage'. Note the word 'serious': without it, a wrongdoer could often get the boat he failed to avoid disqualified along with himself. There are often times when the only way of proving you had right of way and were baulked is by causing contact. Note too that a yacht luffing is expressly allowed to make contact. The reasoning here is that both luffer and luffed will be moving in the same direction and hence contact will be comparatively harmless. This is demonstrated in Rule 34, which is intended to make clear that the right-of-way yacht must not baulk the other in her attempt to keep clear.

Rule 35 asks – rather than instructs – that the right-of-way yacht should always hail to make her intentions clear, but

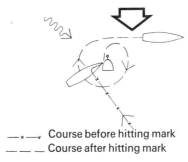

—×— **Course before hitting mark**
— — — **Course after hitting mark**

If you hit a mark: when a mark is touched it is only necessary, when Rule 45 is in force, to loop around it before continuing. But during this time the boat must give way to all others regardless of which tack she is on. Normal rights are not regained until you have drawn clear of the mark.

absolves the luffing yacht from this requirement.

At the other end of our so-called 'corpus' we have Rule 46, which makes it clear that yachts in a race which have anchored, capsized or gone aground still have their rights.

Rule 49 is one of those universal cries from the soul which one could use on almost any occasion. Therefore it is good that half of it should be taken up by saying that yachts may be disqualified under it only if no other rule applies and only if the violation is clear-cut. The other half of this rule, the meaty half, declares that a yacht shall attempt to win a race only 'by fair sailing, superior speed and skill'. This makes it clear that you must not paddle with your hands over the lee side, or

115

switch on your engine after dark, or drill a hole in the bottom of your rival.

The latest (1973) rules aim to reduce rule abuse. For this reason there is a new rule 74 which for the first time permits a Race Committee to exclude a competitor from further racing in a series because of 'gross breach of good manners or sportsmanship'.

The rules, as I have said, go on and on, and there are whole books totally devoted to them. Here there is only space for the essentials. You cannot hope to become a rule expert overnight,

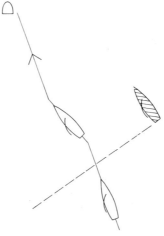

Misleading—legally: you are just laying the mark on starboard tack but you do not want to telegraph this fact to the boat behind, on port tack. So when this other boat crosses your stern and looks across to judge how you are heading, you take care to bear off for a few seconds. This will persuade the boat behind to continue on port and overstand.

but you should aim to achieve an easy, relaxed relationship with them so that as any common racing situation develops and no matter how quickly it might develop, you should be able to use the rules to your own advantage, first to avoid an incident or collision and secondly to avoid yielding unnecessary ground tactically. This does demand a knowledge of the rules that isn't often found, not even among Olympic contenders. The truth is that rules themselves discourage the sort of familiarity that I have said is necessary. They are formidably, almost invincibly complex, and they do not seem to be improving with time and modification.

116

There is one other matter which is closely related to the rules. That is the business of protesting. A protest in yacht racing is equivalent to an appeal for leg before wicket in cricket. There is a misconception, more common in some quarters than others, but tending to run in schools, which views protesting as unsporting.

The fact is that some protests are going to be inevitable if the rules are to be properly observed. This is because the rules themselves are so complicated that there are bound to be times when crews will have different views of the same incident. If this incident involved contact between yachts, or the impeding of one yacht which feels aggrieved, the only proper way out is to examine all the evidence and get the decision of experts in a protest hearing. For this to come about, the aggrieved crew must hoist a protest flag in their rigging as soon after the protest as possible. (This is normally a plain red flag but any flag signal will usually do.) The next job is to ensure that the crew of the boat you are protesting against is informed that you are protesting. They may well retire on hearing this, which will mean you don't have to bother further, but if they feel they were in the right, you must follow your protest through. On returning to shore you inform the race committee of your intention to protest. This done, you then write out the protest, sometimes using an official form. This must contain all the circumstances of the incident, the names of the yachts, the race, the date of the race, and most important, the rules believed infringed. Diagrams often help to amplify the words.

This written protest is then lodged with the protest committee, sometimes with a fee (to guard against frivolous protests, it is said) who will announce a time and place for the hearing. Protestor and protestee will be well advised to bring witnesses, if possible from outside their own yachts. If the evidence is found and agreed by the committee or jury, it shouldn't be difficult for them to come to a verdict. If they cannot agree on evidence they should dismiss the case, though there is a tendency to disqualify too readily and often to disqualify both parties in a contact.

If one party still feels aggrieved over a matter which does not concern the evidence so much as the judgment of the committee, a further, ultimate recourse is still open. Either party can appeal to his National Authority. There are certain appeal cases of this sort which are welcomed by authorities since they do serve as precedents and point up and clarify dubious points. But if only the rules weren't so horribly complicated none of this pseudo-legal carry on would be necessary (and a number of committee men would be kept from their favourite hobby).

The optional lesser penalties (20° penalty or 720° turn) introduced for 1973 are intended to reduce the number of protests.

Remember above all that with the continued growth in popularity of the sport, the size of racing fleets and the number of beginners, there has been an unfortunate slackening in recent years, in the general standard of rule observance. For years, I preached the cause of more give and take in the racing rules. Certainly there is no fun to be had from your racing if each start makes you feel as if you are entering a courtroom. Yet I have to admit that no sooner was more give and take accepted than more crass rule-breaking occurred. Some small class races have recently come very close to real mayhem. The protest hearing is infinitely more civilized, even if more time-consuming, than the paddle used to strike a rival.

If there is not to be a nasty backlash which will make us all the unwilling slaves of these wordy rules, each one of us must watch his step, throughout the next race and every race after that.

8 You Against the Rest – 1

Start and first beat

It may be stating the obvious to say that your sailing boat depends upon a supply of wind to sustain her momentum, but an unhampered wind supply is something that has to be schemed for, fought for, nursed and at all times stoutly defended. In fact one can say that the first principle of yacht racing is to get clear air for your sails. With clear air you can prove your mettle; without it you will be fighting with one hand tied behind your back or, more accurately, fighting while choking for breath. If you can keep a clear supply of wind from start to finish you will almost certainly win out over your rivals, for few will go right through a race with many competitors without having his wind starved or taken for at least part of the time.

Fighting for your wind

Getting clear air may sound defensive and negative, but it will sometimes call for aggression. Thus it is that you will need to show aggression at the start if you are to cross the line with your wind clear, and it is the need for clear air that makes the start of any race so important. In this context one may say that where a running race ends with a sprint, a yacht race begins with a sprint, for it is in those first few moments before and after the starting gun that the fate of the whole race is very often decided, and it is decided so soon because this is when the cards are dealt, some getting clear winds, others finding themselves panting for air to leeward of the sails of countless others.

First then, our action must be to fight to win clear wind. Second – but only very secondarily – you should think of ways in which to take away the wind from others' sails. This aspect

119

of a clear wind is far less important than the first because in the one case you are looking after one suit of sails, your own, but in the other, unless the affair is a two boat match race, you have to try to take wind from the sails of everyone of your rivals and this is a tall order. So it is much more profitable to try to go as fast as you can yourself than to slow others down.

As a race approaches the end, then slowing others down, either by taking their wind or by some other subterfuge, becomes more realistic, for at this stage it is often possible to see which rivals are real threats and which are not. This leads us to a second axiom: always keep between the next mark and your most dangerous opponent. It might be more helpful to say simply: always keep between the finishing line and your most dangerous opponent. It will hardly ever be possible until the end of a series to tell who is your most dangerous rival.

Axiom number three might be: sail the fastest, which will nearly always be the shortest, course. Though half the fascination of racing is all that zig-zagging about, one should not allow this to blind one to the basic simple fact that the best way of getting between A and B is to ride the straight line (and why should this be called a bee-line when bees in fact seem to dilly-dally in the most haphazard way?) But the truth is that far too many racing sailors spend far too much of their time off the bee-line. One has only to think of luffing.

Don't lose the finish

Axiom number four: only relax after the finishing line is finally crossed. The wind and the water being what they are – untamed and almost unpredictable – no lead, however long, is ever completely safe and no bit of sheer luck is ever completely free from the risk that it might be as quickly taken away as granted. No wind, however steady, will blow for ever. Work as hard downwind as up, work as hard along the final leg as along the opening one. Work as hard when you are lying next to last as when lying second. And here, we can stress the need for the very necessary 'killer instinct', of which mention was made in the opening chapter.

Flying Dutchmen at the start of their one windy race in the 1972 Olympics at Kiel. BL 44 (Brazil) capsized when she tacked within seconds of this picture but recovered well to finish tenth. Britain's Rodney Pattison, the overall winner, pulled up to third in this race, though he appears buried in this picture (almost hidden by MX122).

Jack Knight

Starting

Let us now go back to before the beginning. You will be wise to get out to the race course early, to give yourself plenty of time in which to sniff out the wind, use gadgets or simple observation to pry out the currents, check up on course instructions and race signals, and not least important, find out all about the starting line.

There is, on every starting line, a best part for starting from, and the longer the line the more vital it is that you should determine this part accurately. That is why the starts in championship races, with their huge fleets and quarter-mile lines, are so critical.

The line

People sometimes describe a line carelessly. They often talk about 'the windward end' when they mean no more than the

121

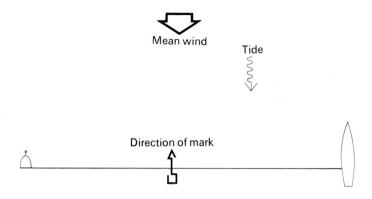

Mean wind

Tide

Direction of mark

Such a perfectly laid start line is very rare. On the line above a perfect start can be made anywhere along it, but most people will go for the starboard end, so consider alternatives. Do not attempt a port tack start unless the line is very long and the fleet relatively small. The snag to a centre of the line start is the difficulty of estimating when one is right on the line. In practice, as below, the start line is hardly ever perfect because of shifts from the mean wind. The line may not be at right angles to the course to the first mark; the tide may be out of line or varying in strength along the line. Usually there is a combination of these factors which take time and good judgement to assess correctly.

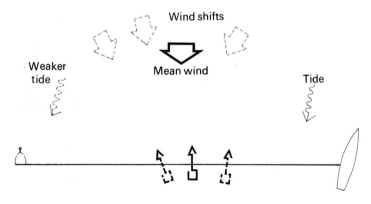

Wind shifts

Mean wind

Weaker tide

Tide

committee boat or shore end of the line. The windward end of a line is the end nearest to the direction from which the wind is blowing, and will normally be the preferred end from which to start.

Traditionally, races are started whenever possible to wind-

122

ward. The idea of this is that the first leg should be a beat because a beat sorts out the fleet quickest, so that approaching the first mark there will be less likelihood of dangerous bunching. If a race is started on a square run, the chances are that the fleet will get to the first mark in a great jam, for nobody will have been able to draw clear of the pack – no sooner does one boat pick up a flaw of wind and skitter ahead a bit than she runs into the wind shadow cast by those she left behind and slows down once more.

Race officers mostly aim to set the start at right angles to the wind so that the first leg will be a dead beat into the eye of the wind. If the wind is perfectly true, if the starting mark anchorers do their work accurately, and if the wind remains steady, a perfectly square line may be obtained and then it won't matter at all whether you start at one end or the other, or in the middle. But there are too many 'ifs' in this equation. The wind hardly ever stays steady; the anchorers hardly ever drop the hooks exactly in the right place. Often a current will upset them, or the eyesight of the race officer directing them. Almost always one end of a supposedly true line will be biased over the other end; i.e. will be to windward, however slightly, of the other.

The favoured end

Some clever race officers attempt to favour the outer end of the line (the end furthest from their station) and deliberately give a bias to the line. They know very well that for safety's sake, in a large start, wise sailors will start on the right-of-way starboard tack, no matter what part of the line they will be starting from. Since they will all be coming in from right to left, they will naturally tend to start well above the right hand end of the line, and come swooping in close to the right hand limit mark. Then if they are early they can run down the line, using up time while always being close to crossing. But if the line is swung around a little so that the left hand or outer end is favoured, this will encourage the alert to start well away from the right hand end and will help to spread the fleet more evenly along the line's length.

There are several ways in which you can calculate which end is favoured. One way is to arrange with a friendly rival for both of you to make a practise start, at the same moment, from opposite ends and on opposite, converging tacks. You should soon be able to see which boat is gaining on the other. But doing this, you do show your hand to others who may be watching you. You can sail up to leeward of the flags flying at each end and see how they point. You can luff head to wind on the line and try to judge what sort of an angle you are making with the line. More accurately, if more dangerously, you can reach along the line with your jib flapping and your mainsail sheeted to the exact centre of its track, cleated and just full of wind – almost on the point of lifting. When you have reached along the line for a few score yards and adjusted the sail accurately you put about, without touching the mainsheet, and sail back along the reciprocal course. If the sail is now lifting you know that you are headed towards the favoured end. If it seems unduly pinned in and its set would be improved by easing the sheet, you know you are sailing away from the favoured end.

Of course the end favoured for wind direction will not always be the favoured end for winning the race. The start may be laid at right angles to the shore and the first leg sailed against a strong current which will be less strong closer to the shore. The favoured end for the wind's direction may be the offshore end, but it may well pay to start from the inshore end so that you are free to put about quickly after the gun and head into the shore on port tack and so get into the slack water first.

There is another, more worrying, fact about the so-called favoured end. Put yourself in the position of the race officer. Presumably he has worked very carefully to make the line as square as possible or else to give it a slight port hand end bias. If the line suddenly becomes more strongly biased to the port end, or conversely, suddenly favours the starboard end, you may take it that the wind has shifted. Now if it is one of those

A start in the 1971 Tempest World Championships at Marstrand in north Sweden. The author in *Bad News* K58 goes for the leeward position and will be able to foot off, once clear of the line, in order to seize a safe leeward berth on G35 and others further to windward.

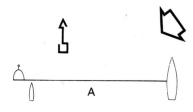

A

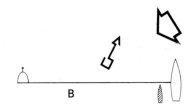

B

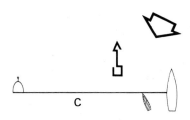

C

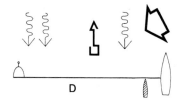

D

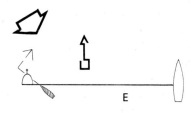

E

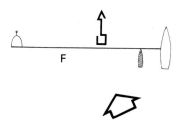

F

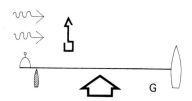

G

Picking the favoured end: here are various examples of differing conditions at the start, with the standard symbols for wind, direction to next mark and tide. Two wavy arrows (D) show stronger tide at one end than the other. The position of the shaded boat indicates the favoured starting position, but it should be noted that other boats are not allowed for here. In A, for instance, with a free wind start at the leeward end, making sure of a clear wind and hitting the line at speed is vital, or a large fleet may come along and chop your wind completely. In E the port tack is better, but it is safest to cross the line on starboard, flinging onto port as soon as you have checked that it is safe days when the wind is shifting rhythmically about 10 degrees either side of a mean direction – a most common occurrence – you may rest assured that the race officer will have already detected that mean direction. Therefore, if it has shifted to one side don't rush in to start at the now favoured end until you have satisfied yourself that the wind isn't about to swing rhythmically back to the other extreme. If this happens, you will find yourself steadily lifted up as you begin the first beat, and gradually more and more rivals will appear to weather of you. The safe thing to do, if you still elect to start at the

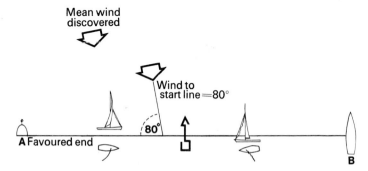

Here are two ways of judging wind direction on the start line. (1) Sail parallel to the line with jib off and mainsail trimmed correctly for the wind. Then put about to sail the reciprocal course with the mainsheet exactly as before. If the main is too far out you are sailing towards the favoured end. With the wind as shown you discover that A is the favoured end. (2) By compass. Take the compass course when sailing parallel to the line. Now luff head to wind and take a compass reading of the wind direction. If the difference is less than 90 degrees you were sailing towards the better end, if more than 90 degrees, you were sailing away from it.

temporarily favoured end, is to tack across the fleet just as soon as possible after starting. Then you will stand to gain as the wind does its rhythmic swing. But you must realise that if you start on starboard tack from the port end and the wind starts to lift you up, it is very unlikely that you will be able to cross ahead of many when you attempt to put about onto port to cross to the starboard wing.

This is why I said it is important to get out to the start early and smell out the wind. It may take fully twenty minutes to get an insight into whether the wind is steady, shifting rhythmically about a mean direction, or veering or backing steadily.

As a line gets longer and longer it becomes more and more difficult to tell when you are right up on it. That is why it helps to start at one end or the other. Some race officers are beginning to introduce middle marks, which are a great help in this respect. On accurately set lines there is often much to be said for starting in the middle of the line, if you can only judge

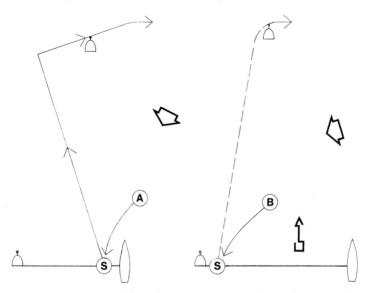

Starting: when the wind blows from one side of the course it pays to start from that end of the line, so long as the first leg remains a beat to windward. The best end here is at A, on starboard tack.

As soon as the wind so strongly favours this end that the leg becomes a fetch, the opposite end of the line at B will pay since it will provide a faster sailing course and will keep you clear of luffing and mutually interfering boats.

the line itself from this point. The chances are that there will be fewer boats and hence more clear wind hereabouts. And you will be in a fine springboard position from which you can leap, either to port or starboard, as soon as you begin to be able to see which wing is being favoured. In England one often hears talk of long lines 'bulging' in the middle. In my experience, the reverse is more often the case. On most long starts, there is a

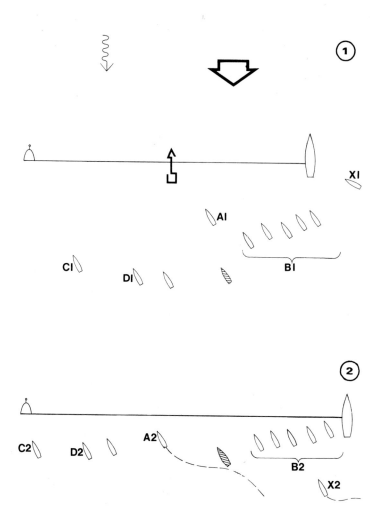

great sag in the middle of the starting line, with boats attempting to start in the middle often as much as ten boat lengths back from the line. This is because at sea level it is quite impossible to tell, by looking each side of you, whether the line is straight or curved; you can tell only whether you are ahead of or behind those close to you. So give a thought to starting bravely in the middle and ahead of the general line. If you can

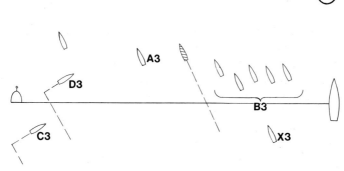

If other boats have secured the best windward positions at the start, try to win yourself clear wind to leeward. You can sometimes do this by coming in fast and a little late on the line where you see another boat has been early and has had to bear away down the line. Encourage people who want to bear away across you to do so, as it will help to leave the hole you want, but don't do it yourself. In (1) the people at the weather end (B1) are not going flat out because they are afraid of being early, and are chopping each other's wind. Boat A1 is clearly early. Follow him in until he has to bear away, giving him the opportunity to do so (2) and go flat out for the line. You now have a little space to bear away which enables you to go fast enough to clear your wind on Group B1 (3). Boats C and D, for reasons of their own, were making a port-end start, with the idea of getting in a quick port tack to start beneath the fleet, which might or might not pay. C has failed completely, but D has done it well – if it is a good thing to do.

Always avoid starting immediately to weather of a boat that you know is specially good to windward. Boat X, which is trying to force a passage in round the committee boat, has quite rightly been told by the weather boat of Group B to buzz off, and can only fall in lamely astern, tacking to clear his wind when he can.

first of all check this point by transits to high landmarks or moored vessels, so much the better.

In small boats do not set too much store by carefully timed, dummy runs away from and back up to the line. The trouble with these is that the actual start is likely to take place in much more confused wind, so that you will then take longer than on the dummy run.

Many skippers have the bad habit of getting too near a line too soon. You should time your start, not to cross the actual line on the gun but to cross a point a few yards short of the line with a few seconds remaining. This gives you some leeway and should enable you to accelerate over the last few seconds. The bad thing about our modern, highly crowded big regatta starts is the almost hysterical feeling that spreads like an epidemic through the fleet, that unless you book your place on the line with a minute or so to go, you will never be able to sail into the front rank at all. If only enough people observed the rules carefully, this feeling would be quickly found to be quite false, for the rules give the right of way to the boat coming up from behind and converging from leeward. Up to gunfire such a boat is fully entitled to luff others gradually (but not beyond closehauled and not in a way that does not permit them to take avoiding action). But he can come up gradually and he should call 'Water' or 'Up, up' the while. Those people right up on the line, flapping their sails and tillers and tongues, quite dead in the water, are really quite vulnerable – sitting ducks. But they do usually have safety in numbers.

The planned start

In large craft your start will need to be more fully and tightly pre-planned, with your approach manoeuvres explained to the crew beforehand. In smaller, more reactive boats you should play it more loosely and flexibly, watching for last minute openings. Many good starting skippers have a happy knack of making a big space directly to leeward of them so that once they start they can knock off a point or two, to get up to full speed more quickly, without falling into anybody's back wind. I am addicted to starting from the port end so that I can sail as full as I like on starboard tack. But I must say that this start lets me down almost as often as it pulls me through. It has become too much of a habit.

If you do try this port end start, you can often gain the initiative by sailing in fast on port tack and then putting about fast, close under the lee bow of the nearest starboard tacker. By doing this you surprise him and give him back wind, but you

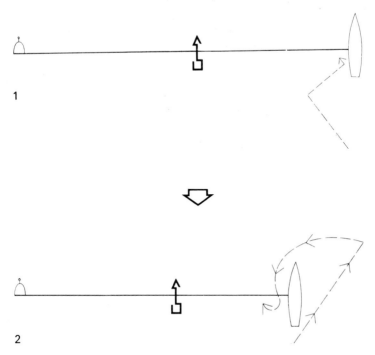

Two risky but effective starts which can be made where a large committee vessel
is used. Of course (2) is not possible in the case of the one-minute or
five-minute rules being applied by the sailing committee, a practice which is
increasing.

will find yourself short of line if he is already a trifle early.
Sometimes it will be best to pass under the nearest starboard
tacker, or even several boats, before tacking into a space. Try to
look ahead, so that if you find yourself in a difficult position
with ten seconds or so to go, you escape from it before the
situation becomes desperate. One often sees a group of boats
being carried willy-nilly the wrong side of the outer mark by a
strong foul tide. Bear off sharply, slip away from the group,
then gybe around and look for other avenues of opportunity.

Not all starts are to windward. Often clubs have fixed lines
with transits on shore. At Cowes, so-called Mecca of yachts-

men, the host clubs commonly give reaching starts away to the east or the west. Such starts are usually even more difficult than windward ones and need more careful pre-planning. If you start to windward, on a reaching start, you may get more wind to begin with but you may soon find yourself irrevocably drawn into a luffing match which nobody wins, certainly not you. If you more daringly start to leeward, you will have to be sure to hit the line at the gun, at full speed. Otherwise you may never smell a clear wind. And from this end you may not be able to carry a spinnaker. On the other hand you may, by pointing higher, actually sail faster or even get onto a plane,

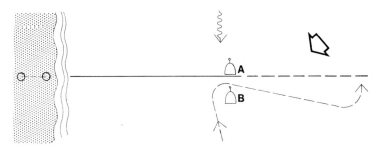

With a starting line consisting of a shore transit, the buoy marking the outer end of the line may have been carried the wrong side of the line by a change of tide, or it may have been badly set in the first place. The proper position of the buoy is at A, but the tide has carried it back to B. You can take legitimate advantage of this by sailing between the mark and the line before the start though you may have to explain your actions in the protest room afterwards. Race officers should always take care to see that outer marks lie on the course side of the line to guard against this.

which will be denied those sailing more broadly. If the start is a square run you should do what you can to carve a clear path away from all others, up the first leg. It won't matter whether this is to port or starboard. In fact with a very big fleet in a lightish wind, you won't even have to bother to be on the line at all at the gun, for you will almost certainly run up and blanket those ahead.

Remember that you are nowadays allowed to touch the starting marks (unless the race instructions specifically state otherwise) but having touched you must re-round them in an outward direction, i.e. anticlockwise at the port end, clockwise

at the starboard end. You will have to circle the committee
boat if there is no inner mark at this end. Any tender or dinghy
moored to the committee boat counts as part of it.

Starts should be fun. In small races at any rate, take a few
risks; use some dash and daring, think of Nelson.

The windward leg

Now, at last, the gun has gone, there has been no recall, and we
are faced with the first leg, which for our purposes we will

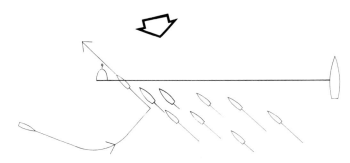

An effective start when the wind favours the port end is to approach late, on
port tack, and put about under the lee bow of the nearest starboard tack
approacher. This takes the initiative from him, but you will be in trouble if the
leeward starboard tackers are approaching early. You may also have trouble if
others besides yourself plan this start. If they do, make sure that you come in
after them, not before.

assume to be to windward. We will also assume the current is
irrelevant (but so often it is a factor).

The first thing is to clear your precious clear air. You are
unlikely to do this by tacking repeatedly after the gun. This will
only slow you just as it is necessary to make a sprint. Lesser
helmsmen often tack to clear their wind on one boat, only to
find they have put themselves under another. So they have to
tack a second time, and so on and so on.

'Kill, kill, kill' – as soon as you have a chance of running
over somebody to leeward, taking his wind and forcing him to
tack, do so. Don't try to squeeze up; you will only lose speed

135

and make more leeway, ending up further to leeward and further behind.

Unless you are very sure of yourself, do not immediately head for the extreme wing on either side. Start looking for heading wind shifts. Every time you are freed you are being hurt, for there will be others on your weather quarter who will be freed too and they will then tend to move up on your weather beam.

Use of compass

This is where a good compass is of immense benefit, even in a small dinghy. If you did not get cleanly away and are surrounded by other boats, it will be very difficult to detect a wind shift, for you will not have a clear view of the coastline or horizon ahead. But by checking your compass you will be able to tell any header of 10 degrees or more, and any shift of this order is well worth taking advantage of. Just how often you will tack on headers will depend on the size of your boat and her handiness in stays; also on the character of the wind.

All things being equal, try to get on the tack which is presently pointing closest to the weather mark. If you are on this tack already and the wind frees, you may find yourself practically fetching the mark. If the wind heads you on this tack you will put about and may then find you are again on the tack which points closest to the mark.

It is much easier, trying to sail this first beat well, if you have got away among the first few boats. Wind shifts will be more easily detected; your tactical position in the fleet will be much more obvious. You will even be able to see the weather mark sooner and more easily. You should always tack with this mark's position very much in mind.

The only time you should go straight out to the lay line on this first beat is when you are sure of a good reason for doing so. If racing in a bay, past experience may tell you to expect a wind bend which will head you as you close with the shore. Therefore you take this shorewards tack from the line, riding it all the way, past the first point at which you were headed until you feel you are well into the new, shore-influenced wind.

136

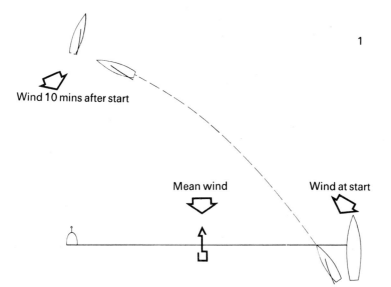

Wind 10 mins after start

Mean wind

Wind at start

Cashing in on rhythmic wind shifts at the start: quite commonly a wind will shift regularly about 10 degrees each side of a mean direction. The good race officer will lay his line at right angles to this mean. If at the moment of starting one end is favoured, the chances are that before very long the wind will shift back again, through and past the mean.

To take fullest advantage of this you should start at the favoured end and then make every effort to sail across to the other wing. In (1) you start on starboard, at the starboard end, and hold onto your starboard tack even though you are headed, until finally, when you do tack, you will be to port of the fleet and first to get the favouring shift.

In (2), when the fleet is too threatening to make anything but a starboard tack start impossible, you begin looking for a hole to get in a port tack as soon as you can. Hold onto this tack, again even when at first you are headed, until you are over on the starboard side ready to gain more than you have lost when the rhythmic shift comes in.

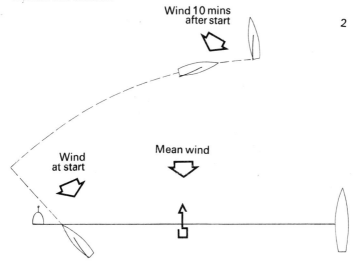

Wind 10 mins
after start

2

Wind
at start

Mean wind

Then you tack and lo! – the rest of the fleet is to leeward of you and you feel twenty-one again and a king to boot.

Sometimes, racing in the afternoon at a place like San Diego for instance, you will head to the right from the start because you will know that the daily sea breeze will follow the sun and veer as you sail on so that you will be gradually, ever so gradually, headed. Then you put about just short of the lay line and again lo! – you later find yourself lifted right up to it on starboard right-of-way tack.

A further reason for going to the layline, but a much riskier one, is to head offshore to meet an incoming sea breeze. From what coastal racing I have done, I would say this is a considerably less favourable bet than heading inshore for the wind bend. What is so risky here is the timing. If the sea breeze hadn't come in before the start, who knows whether it will announce itself just at the moment you choose to sail out to embrace it? More often than not, race starts in British coastal waters are delayed to await the sea breeze. Once it has arrived one can only expect it to freshen and veer during the day.

On this first leg do not worry about covering others. Worry only about sailing fast yourself. This even goes for points series and final races of points series. There will be plenty of time later on in the race for defensive covering.

The weather mark

As you approach the mark, give a thought to the tack on which you wish to pass it. Of course the safe approach tack in large fleets is the starboard tack, but in a fleet of a hundred there is going to be a continuous procession of starboard tackers parading past the mark for minutes on end. The odd skipper who hopes to be able to come in on port, find a gap and pop around, is going to be taking a very big risk indeed. And yet, risks like this do sometimes come off. The alternative entails having to sail towards the mark from a long way off, on a long starboard tack, with your wind taken not just by one boat but by scores. As you near the mark the wind will get more and more confused, and you will find yourself sailing less and less

138

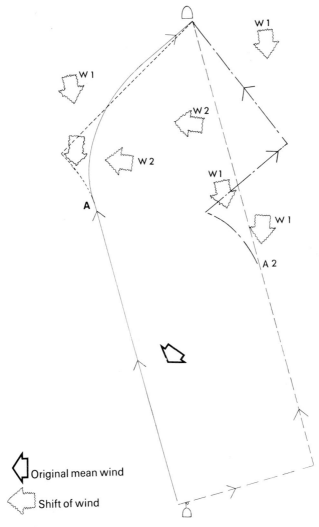

W 1

W 1

W 2

W 2

W 1

A

W 1

A 2

Original mean wind

Shift of wind

Planning the windward leg: you should always sail first on the tack that takes you closest to the next mark. The broken and continuous lines show the choice of courses when faced with a long-and-short tack beat. Whether the wind frees or backs the continuous-line path is best. If a wind shift covers the whole area at the same time it will reach the two courses illustrated at A and A2. If the wind frees (W2) the boat on the broken line, he will have overstood, but the other boat can just luff up to the mark. If at A and A2 the wind heads (W1), the boat shown by the continuous line need only sail a short distance on a headed course before putting about and laying the mark on the other tack. If the boat on the broken line does this he will find himself a long way to leeward of the mark and also of the other boat.

Even if the wind remains perfectly steady for the whole leg of the course, the continuous line will still be preferable, for it will be easier for the helmsman to judge when to tack to lay the mark. The boat on the broken line has to judge when to tack from a much greater distance. The wind shifts are shown exaggerated for emphasis, but such vivid wind shifts do sometimes occur.

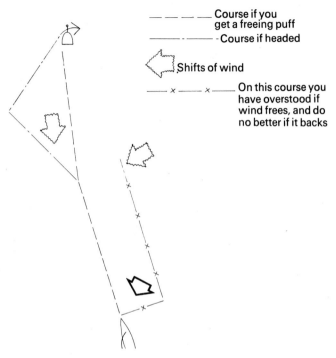

Course if you get a freeing puff

─── · ─── · ─── · - Course if headed

Shifts of wind

─── x ─── x ─── On this course you have overstood if wind frees, and do no better if it backs

When not quite laying a mark from a long distance off, do not put in a hitch to windward, and tack only when very severely headed. A freer, later, will lift you up to the mark from your old course, and the hitch will then have proved unnecessary. A severe header will enable you to lay the mark on the other tack.

high. If you thought you were just laying the mark from a hundred yards back, you will now find you are well below it.

Therefore, if lying well back in a big fleet, overstand the mark on port before tacking onto starboard. You may lose three boats but gain a dozen – for at least a dozen will be caught understanding near the mark and will have to tack across frantically – often fouling right-of-way rivals.

In these important races and big fleets you will find the air more and more cut up as you close the weather mark. Mostly this is to do with the number of spectator boats positioned to windward of it. It may also have something to do with another class which has only just rounded ahead of your fleet. It seems to me that if the wind is harassed too much it sometimes

140

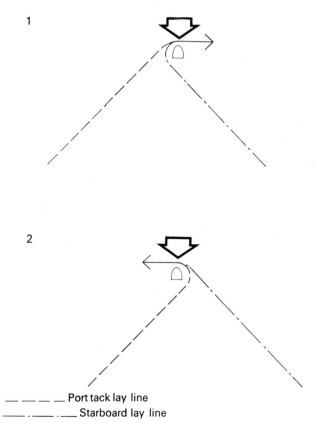

1

2

— — — — Port tack lay line
——— · ——— · — Starboard lay line

Approaching the first weather mark: you need to keep in mind the positions of the lay lines for each tack, and the slight change in positions according to whether you are leaving the mark to starboard, as (1) or to port (2). Principles to follow when rounding a weather mark at any time are: (i) keep a clear wind, (ii) never go right out to the lay lines too early, (iii) with a large fleet, normally approach on starboard tack, even though when leaving a buoy to starboard it means a tack, (iv) if you are leaving the mark to port, starboard tack approach is even more to be recommended.

decides to give up altogether, and simply downs tools and skulks out. This is another reason for overstanding – you will not be able to sail as high in a light, sulky wind as in a good true breeze.

In smaller fleets guard against overstanding, in fact always tack just short of the lay line (unless this puts you under a boat which will be on your weather bow). If you are just short of standing the mark a 'freer' will bring you right up to it. A 'header' can only be taken advantage of by tacking.

On the weather leg never tack unless there is a good positive reason for doing so – either to clear your wind, cash in on a header, lee bow, cover an opponent, or tack for the mark.

Try not to let your own tactics be dictated by others. Thus it will normally be preferable when on port tack to bear up and pass under the stern of a starboard tacker, rather than to put about under his lee bow and find yourself herded off in the direction that the starboard tacker, and not you, wants to go.

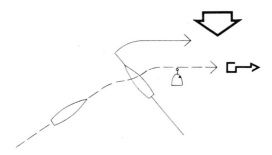

If close to a mark on port tack with a little in hand, and approached by a boat on starboard claiming rights, shout to him to hold his course. Once you begin to bear away to avoid him he may not tack to baulk you, but must continue clear across you. You can often use this right in other tight situations, such as at a finish.

Conversely, it is often better to encourage a port tacker to sail clear across you and continue on his course, even if you have to bear off for him a little, than to have him tack on your lee bow from where he will be dowsing you with his used up air. But make sure he understands you, by hailing early and loud 'Hold your course' or 'Carry on, you are OK'.

Approaching the mark be alert to the very real peril of not being able to lay and not being able to tack, because of the proximity of a boat behind you and slightly to weather. You should see this situation developing and respond by pinching as high as possible so that the boat behind falls down to leeward. If this fails you must hope that he too will fail to lay. But if he can lay and looks set to do so, your option is to bear

142

off, turn through 270 degrees and gybe, hoping to cross in the gap behind the boat that got you into trouble. Your salvation here is foresight – see a tricky situation like this before it becomes reality.

In a seaway one tack may be better angled to the waves so that the boat will make better speed over the ground. If this is so be very careful when trying to cross boats on this tack when you are on the opposite tack.

A final word on tactics up the first weather leg (we shall consider the defensive tactics of lee bowing and windward covering on the ultimate windward leg): your plans will be influenced by the type of event. If this is a single important

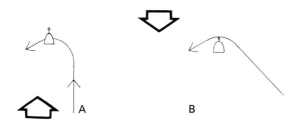

A   B

Rounding marks: normally you should do as much of your turn as you can before you reach the mark, departing on your new course from as close to it as possible (A). Practise rounding marks whenever you can. In (B) remember to leave enough space to enable you to ease the boom out progressively to get the added acceleration, without touching the mark with it.

race, such as the Prince of Wales Cup for International 14s, you should be more inclined to take a gamble and shape your tactics boldly.

If, as is more likely nowadays, this single race is only part of a longer series, a stepping stone to greater things, you should be less ready to take risks, more willing to hedge your bets and settle for a mean, middle of the road, safety-first course. The trouble with the bold course to one wing or the other is that if it fails it is likely to fail calamitously and leave you nearly last. The middle of the road course will hardly ever put you worse than the middle – a position from which you should be able to build a respectable finish in the first 10 per cent of the fleet. Ten per centers often win week-long series.

9 You against the Rest – 2

From the first mark On

Rounding a weather mark is always difficult, the more so if the fleet is large, the competition good and the boats closely spaced. The prime problem is that you are having to bear off, moving your sails further away from the wind so that the pressure upon them at first decreases. The difficulties are heightened if you are at the same time trying to set a spinnaker.

The first tip is to bear off gradually, turning your rudder slowly and easing your sheets sparingly, in order that your boat decelerates as little as possible. Approach the mark a little wide with a good head of steam, and make sure you are already bearing away and hence inscribing your turning circle well before you come abreast the mark. In this way you should end up to windward of others nearby, and this is vital. Particularly with fast planing types such as the 505, Flying Dutchman and Tornado catamaran, it is very easy to lose yards and yards by bearing off, slowing the boat and getting to leeward of others behind, who may be luffing up, increasing speed, accelerating and moving over your clear wind.

Use of spinnaker

We are assuming here that after rounding the weather mark you will find the next leg to be a broad reach, Olympic style. If the course is at all accurately laid and the wind at all steady, you can be confident that you will be able to carry a spinnaker. We will go into hoisting procedures in a special chapter, but suffice to say here that it is no good rushing up the spinnaker if it is only going to flap and flog once up, while your crew wrestles to get the pole in place, the uphaul and downhaul rigged and the guy and sheet roughly adjusted. Better to do these routine jobs first, delaying the spinnaker hoist until it can go up and begin

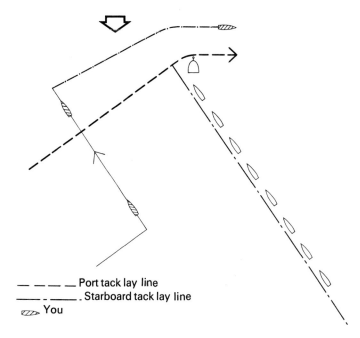

— — — — Port tack lay line
——— · ——— Starboard tack lay line
〰️ You

Approaching the weather mark: if there is a solid procession of boats developing on starboard, don't drop into it. You will lose a lot on any boat that has
clear wind and water. Overstand the port lay line and approach on port, clear
of the procession. Then you only lose a little.

to fill immediately. On three-man boats it is best to approach
the mark on the tack upon which the subsequent reach will be
sailed; then the pole can be rigged and guyed before the mark
is reached, so that the spinnaker can be sent up right on the
buoy. On two-man boats this is not often possible.

Keep to weather while you are sorting things out. Only when
you have your sails full and drawing well and the boat moving
fast again should you begin to wonder about the best course
for the next (gybing) mark.

Deciding your line

As to the pros and cons of straight line, leeward arcing and
windward arcing reaching courses, much will depend upon the

145

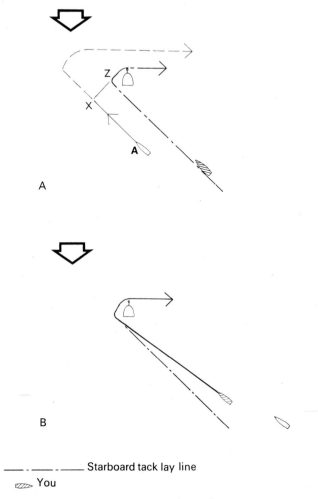

A

B

___ . ___ . ___ Starboard tack lay line

〰️ You

Rounding the weather mark: (A) the wrong way – boat A has sagged off below the lay line and cannot tack at X for the mark because you, astern and to weather, will catch him on port tack. He must lose distance by overstanding as shown in pecked line at Z. (B) the right way – you have clung closely to or even made up above the lay line and can tack, keeping the buoy between you and the following boat, 'scraping him off'.

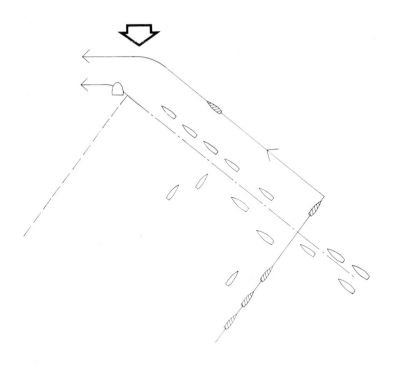

_ _ _ _ _ Port lay line
_____ . _____ . _____ Starboard lay line

🚤 You

If behind in a big fleet and the mark is to be left to port, overstand to starboard
because the wind near the mark will be so cut up that leeway will be excessive.

type of boat you are sailing. If you are in a nimble planing
dinghy with no spinnaker you can sail off to leeward more
resolutely. Your dinghy will respond to puffs quicker and if she
can hit a few planes can double her speed over nearby boats.
So your chances of breaking through to leeward are greatly
increased. If you are racing a displacement keelboat and are
counting on a big spinnaker for most of your speed you will be
far less likely to be able to break through to leeward.

It is essential to plan the tactics of the complete leg from the
start of the leg. It is no good changing your mind halfway. You
will only waste time and lose speed as you luff and bear away.

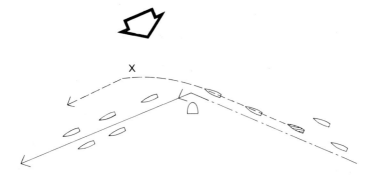

Rounding the weather mark to a reach: before setting the spinnaker in a big fleet it almost always pays to luff out from a mark. Later you can decide to bear away below the crowd, but only when the spinnaker is drawing well and maximum speed has been attained. Luff out and delay hoisting the spinnaker until you are at point X. The crew can be readying pole and guys meanwhile.

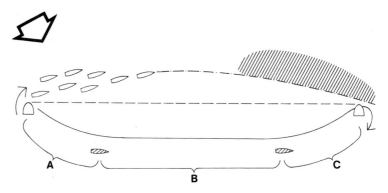

After the weather mark: take care when rounding a mark onto a reach not to get into a group being edged up to weather by boats luffing to clear their wind. A well-timed 'bear away' to below the direct line to the next mark pays off provided you draw well clear (the drawing is not to scale) to ensure a clear wind. You may lose a little distance in section A of the leg, but it will be only a little if boats are getting in each others' way while putting up spinnakers. On section B you are doing better than those boats interfering with each other in the shaded area. On section C you will go a good deal faster because you have luffed onto a closer reach just when boats in the shaded area are bearing away, so slowing down, and also losing more speed because they are taking each others' wind. You also have right of way over all of them as leeward boat until any of them are within two boats' lengths of the mark.

If you reckon that the boats around you are likely to sail the leg badly, allowing themselves to luff each other well to weather and generally squabble amongst themselves instead of getting on with their own individual races, you would be well advised to sheer off to leeward. If this is your decision, stick to it and act decisively. Concentrate at least as hard as you did on the beat. Whenever the wind puffs up, bear off a little more. Whenever the right wave presents itself, ride it off to leeward. Since moving off to leeward of others is inherently a slowing manoeuvre, it should only be attempted in the right circumstances. Yet you have to get far enough to leeward to move out of range of wind shadows.

Coming up to the mark

The benefits of sailing low of the course will only begin to reveal themselves much later, as you approach the next mark. At this stage you will be able to start luffing out a little and hence accelerating, just as the others who have been stoutly

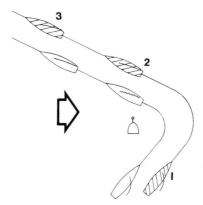

Winning clear wind after rounding: even if a boat has to yield an overlap at a mark all is not lost (1). By rounding close under the lee of the inside boat and taking care to trim sails well and turn smoothly, it should be possible to hold one's speed better than the other boat, which will probably turn too tightly and at first head too high on the new windward leg (2). By romping off slightly when leaving the mark, the outside boat should be able to keep clear air and this, combined with his greater speed, will eventually enable him to squeeze back under the other boat and administer a lee bow (3).

defending their weathers and tending to luff up the whole time will now realise they are high of the mark and must start to bear off.

If, down to leeward, you have managed to keep abreast of those to weather of you, this last-minute ability to luff as you approach the mark and possibly to jump onto a plane or surf a few waves, should take you clear ahead. But remember you have also to come up on a converging course under the sails of those to windward. It is a risk you are taking, but personally I have always been a practising advocate of the leeward reaching course although I have to confess that most of my racing success is achieved on the upwind legs. One thing I am beginning to suspect about several ace helmsmen who habitually take a wide leeward course is that they may be doing this to get far enough away from the opposition so that they can give full rein to their illegal sheet pumping and boat ooching and rolling practices.

One thing against the leeward course – it is less likely to pay if the standard is uniformly high. For in this case your rivals will be unlikely to let themselves be suckered into time-consuming, luffing, cat and dog fights. Wave direction will also have an important bearing on your choice of reaching course. The waves may actually help a boat which is sailing further offwind.

The gybing mark

Gybing the second mark, on our imaginary Olympic course, most of the rules applying to the weather mark will apply again. It is even more important this time to begin your turning arc early so that you will be close to the mark as you *emerge* from your rounding and hence to weather of others. In this case the turn entails a gybe. The way you gybe will depend on your boat and whether or not you are flying a spinnaker. But you should always try to gybe tight enough to finish to windward of those behind. On two-man spinnaker boats, let the sail flog wildly for a few seconds if this means it will be reset sooner. It is only on three-man boats that one can reasonably expect the spinnaker to stay full throughout the gybe.

Remember the racing rules that apply at marks. Once boats come within two lengths of the longer yacht then overlapping conditions govern. To claim an overlap to make an inside turn at a buoy, a skipper must have his overlap before the boat upon which he is making his claim comes within two lengths of the buoy. If the leading boat thinks the claim is wrongly made he must still yield, and protest later. The two-lengths-of-the-mark condition has resulted in skippers claiming very late and dubious overlaps. To prevent this from happening to you it is best to sail into the mark a little high of the proper course, so that you must bear off a little to clear it. This bearing off will tend to break a dubious overlap and prevent others, still more dubious, from ever occurring. But of course it does make it more difficult to end up to weather on the new gybe after the rounding.

In a really big fleet dozens of places can be won and lost at the gybe and skullduggery can pay off. If several boats are being carried to leeward by a slow gyber, or a strong fair tide combined with a light wind, you may seize your chance and gybe inside others with impunity, even though you have no overlap. But if you touch a boat in so doing you must retire – no 'ifs or buts' for you have forced a passage and failed. The bigger the fleet the more important it will be to turn quickly and end up to weather of the crush. Afterwards you can think about shaping a leeward course, but not as you round.

Remember that if you touch the buoy some organizing clubs still require your retirement. Otherwise you may re-round but in so doing you are meant to yield right of way to all others.

We will assume here that this second reaching leg of the course is much higher on the wind than the previous one, and too close for carrying the spinnaker along the entire leg. Along with others, you have been caught out by this and have retained your spinnaker and now find you cannot lay the proper course line. What to do?

The answer will depend upon your type of boat. (I hope you are beginning to see that racing tactics depend very much upon your weapons.) In a moderate or light wind, in a FD, 505, Fireball or 470, I would suggest that you hang on to your spinnaker even though you are taken below the course. Halfway along the leg, or even further if the wind is light, drop the chute quickly and luff up under fore and aft rig for the leeward mark. This will enable you to sail faster through the water, so much faster that you will more than make up for the slight extra distance sailed. In this connection note how little extra distance a 10 degrees veering from the course produces – draw lines with a protractor and measure them if you don't believe me.

In displacement keel boats, even boats as lively as the Tempest, hanging onto a spinnaker is unlikely to pay. You will be unable to sail that much faster unless the wind is very light. Boats will come up to windward of you as you sag below the course with your spinnaker sheet over-tight. These boats will get every puff before you do and will probably ride over your clear wind. It is better therefore to drop the sail even before the mark, though you should be prepared to reset it as you approach the third (the leeward) mark, if the wind has freed or if you have been forced above the course in your efforts to keep a clear wind.

Boats without spinnakers will not have this problem, but skippers will still have to decide whether to keep high or low. Sail the fastest course you can find on the day, but if it is really blowing hard and you can only just lay the mark while keeping your boat upright and footing fast, try to keep a little high of the mark so that you can run off a few degrees and increase speed later. Meanwhile those to leeward of you will be staggering as they begin to luff to make the mark.

The fastest course

Do not worry if in order to get the best from your boat you are forced to sail what a racing motorist would describe as an erratic course. More often than not in sailing, the erratic

Lesson in mark rounding. Finns G1050 and G1041 have taken the mark well, but KZ (New Zealand) 137 and G1049 have approached too close and left their sheet tightening too late, and will start the new weather leg too far to leeward and in the backwind of earlier rivals. Finn Gold Cup, Bermuda.

Bermuda News

course is the fast one. When a big puff causes you to hee overmuch, ease off, even if you find yourself sailing below the course. You will hold your plane and your fast speed longer this way. You may be sure that the puff will die sooner or later and then you can sneak up to windward again. If some big seas roll up from behind, catch the biggest and ride it down to leeward. The secret is to keep your boat at her best.

It is vital to round the leeward mark so that you are fully luffed up, sheeted hard in, and already on the wind as you pass close to the mark and emerge from behind. In order to do this you will have to come into it wide.

Defending a lead

By this late stage in the race, a pattern should have emerged. If you are doing well you will have to spare more tactical thought for the defensive business of covering. If you are leading as you round the mark and are undecided about which tack to sail away on, you should hold on the same tack you rounded the mark on until you have sailed half the length of your lead, then tack. If the second boat continues on the tack on which he passed the mark, you can then tack back a second time, when you will find yourself nicely on his weather. If he tacks quickly around the mark, you should be between him and the next mark, ready to cover.

Your compass should help you decide (neglecting defensive tactics for a moment) which tack is best to start the second beat. This is a critical matter. For if you start off on the wrong tack, you are likely to remain on the wrong foot and be caught on the wrong side of wind shifts for the entire second beat.

The compass is your friend here. If it tells you that you are sailing significantly higher than you were able to do when you sailed on the same tack on the previous beat this is the tack to take – until you are badly headed. If, on the other hand, the compass tells you that you are well below the previous course for this tack then tack quickly.

Of course there are exceptions to this if you know the wind has changed direction since the last beat. It may have changed so much that you can lay the leg on one tack, in which case it would be fatal to go any distance on the other – unless to clear your wind.

From the experience of the first leg it should now be possible to decide which side of the course is better and faster. So you will be more likely on this second windward leg to shape a bold, less tentative course towards one wing or the other, and be less likely to hold to the middle. As a basic rule, never tack all the way to the lay line, and shorten the length of your tacks as you near the mark. The safest way is to sail up the funnel bounded by the two lay lines. In this way you will guard against overstanding because you have gone out to one wing to discover that circumstances have changed and it is not going to pay this time. Do not be too proud to cut your losses, write off the plan and tack back, crossing under the sterns of others. It is often easier to spot a gain on the part of others when you are looking from the losing side. By going still further to the gaining side, under the sterns of some of the early gainers, you may very often end up by gaining more than they did. Again and again I have seen good skippers lose through stubborn refusal to face up to tactical facts realistically. Keep your thinking flexible; as flexible as the wind.

There should not, at this later stage, be quite as much crowding at the weather mark as before. Therefore it should be easier to shape your best approach course with less emphasis on arriving on starboard tack and less need to overstand because of the disturbed wind near the mark.

The square run

Next we are faced with a square run. In many ways this is the most difficult leg, tactically, of the whole race. Small dinghy crews will find this assertion surprising, and indeed it does not really apply to them, as on a run they all often go at roughly equal speed and therefore positions remain much the same as at the previous mark. But for displacement craft with large spinnakers, and such diverse types as multihulls, the run can have a vital effect on final placings.

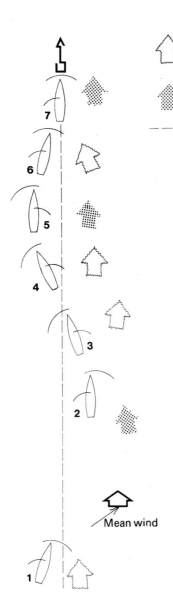

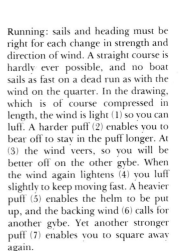

Wind change

Stronger puff

Mean course

Mean wind

Running: sails and heading must be right for each change in strength and direction of wind. A straight course is hardly ever possible, and no boat sails as fast on a dead run as with the wind on the quarter. In the drawing, which is of course compressed in length, the wind is light (1) so you can luff. A harder puff (2) enables you to bear off to stay in the puff longer. At (3) the wind veers, so you will be better off on the other gybe. When the wind again lightens (4) you luff slightly to keep moving fast. A heavier puff (5) enables the helm to be put up, and the backing wind (6) calls for another gybe. Yet another stronger puff (7) enables you to square away again.

Tacking downwind

The first point to grasp is that no sailing boat yet designed likes to sail square down wind. Therefore if the mark is exactly to leeward you should tack down towards it, gybing at least once. In this way you will be able to keep the wind on your quarter and make good speed. The great problem is to arrive at the correct amount of downwind zig-zagging for the type of boat and wind strength. Catamarans may find it best to tack almost as emphatically as if they were sailing upwind. They can sail an extra 45 per cent of the distance and still get ahead, so marked is their acceleration when they luff. But they will only get away with it in a fresh breeze. Other types have surprisingly different characteristics. Offshore boats with their masthead spinnakers and minimal mainsails are happiest when sailed square, although even they like to sail a few degrees high. Solings and Tempests and similar lively keelboats respond less markedly than the catamaran to luffing, but it is still very common in these classes for certain skilful sailors to make more distance on the square run than on any other leg. Remember that the square run leg of the Olympic course is considerably longer than either reach.

Find the best puffs

Once again the plan must be to get clear of other boats in order to win a clear wind path. It is a fact that in the higher levels of yacht racing there is usually a great deal less luffing, scrapping and duelling on the run than in races between less successful and experienced participants. Since on an average Olympic course the run may be close to two miles, boats may well fan out till they are over a half a mile abreast of each other. They may then find themselves running in completely different winds. So the right choice is important. Choose the gybe which will take you closer to the cloud, or to catspaws on the water surface, or to the expectation of an approaching wind. Keep in wind flaws of extra velocity as long as you can by squaring off before them. Then when they pass or fail, luff up to keep your boat's speed. Watch every wave like a hawk. The

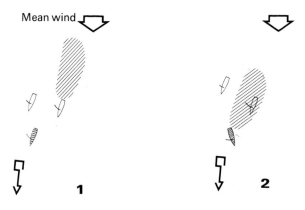

Mean wind

1

2

Defence when running: (1) it is difficult but not impossible to fight off two or more boats close behind when running for a mark or the finish. They have the advantage of getting extra wind streaks first. You must try to split them, then keep between them. Try to luff one beyond the wind axis as the mark is approached, then delay your own gybe so that he crosses your stern. In (1) an extra wind streak is shown shaded, so you luff into it (2). At (3) boat B has gybed to get away while you scrap with the most threatening boat. At (4) the boat astern has gybed to get the right side of the mark, and at (5) you gybe too. (6) shows you rounding the mark, having held both boats off.

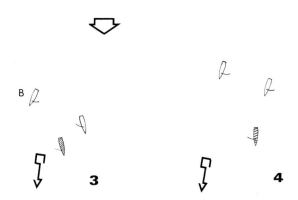

B

3

4

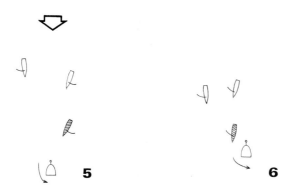

5   6

wave direction, which will not always be in the same direction as the wind, may help you decide which gybe to take from the weather mark. Think of a wave as a ton or more of water being thrown around – that implies there is a great deal of energy somewhere, so why not capture a little of this energy?

The leeward mark

More than on any other part of the course, the approach to the lee mark will dominate your tactical thinking. Since boats tend to bunch on the run, however hard their skippers try to prevent it, it is extremely important that you round close to the buoy and do not have to yield last minute overlaps to others. It is worth dropping back if you find yourself threatened in this manner, so that you can luff across the sterns of others and eventually pick a place near the inside. (This tactic will encounter much more opposition from others than you will gather from the little sketches that Manfred Curry, and many others since, have drawn when recommending it.)

Boats, after a long run, are bound to converge on the mark from all directions, their paths sometimes converging at close to 90 degrees. This and the fact that they will be on opposite tacks, makes the judging of overlaps more difficult than ever. Though starboard tack will hold right of way, a starboard tacker is still obliged to yield an overlap to a port tacker, in the correct circumstances.

159

If under spinnaker, plan your approach so that you can drop the sail on the side from which it will be most conveniently hoisted should you have another downwind leg. Don't be frightened to gybe just short of the mark. Anything is better than slowing up at this vital stage. If the tide is against you, leave your spinnaker up until the last possible moment, but in two-man boats the beginning of the next beat (which is normally the final one) will be the most important consideration, so the gear must be cleared away in order that sails may be sheeted, trapezes hooked up and so on.

As before, unless threatening boats prevent it, approach the lee mark wide so that you can luff up hard, close to the far side of the mark and to windward of less attentive crews. Be careful to see that your crew does not pull in the sheets before it is time, otherwise you will kill the boat's speed and stall the sails.

Hold what you've won

Even more than on the second beat, this third and final leg into the wind and across the finish should be sailed in a defensive spirit – if you arrive at the lee mark well placed.

If you are leading, once again tack as soon as you have sailed half the distance of your lead. If the second place man is comfortably ahead of the third, you should sit on him, even though he appears to be sailing an odd course. Only if the third, or another, really gains should you think of shifting your cover from one boat to another. Remember the simple old maxim: 'always keep between your most dangerous opponent and the finish'.

General cover

It is so much easier if you have a large enough lead to impose general cover. By this I mean that you won't have to worry about sitting on particular boats' wind. You simply have to stay approximately between them and the wind, taking your time when you tack to cover their tack but staying aloof from

160

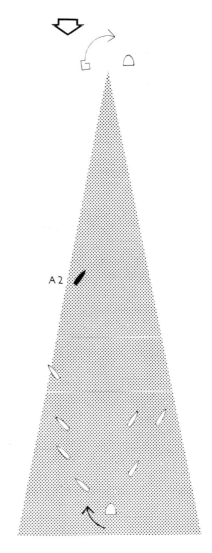

Covering: close cover to windward by tacking to get right on another boat's weather (A) should only be applied late in the race, when you have established a lead and only one boat is a threat. Otherwise loose, or general, cover (A2) is best. It is done by keeping between the opposition and the next mark in the traditional way. Staying in the shaded area enables you quickly to get to a position to apply close cover to any boat that develops into a threat.

incipient tacking duels and giving a good deal more than half your attention to sailing your boat.

Close cover

Close cover is more frantic, more risky, but if your lead is only a few boat lengths, entirely necessary.

In close cover you must be sure that your sails are exactly shadowing the sails of the boat being covered. When he tacks you tack to cover on the instant, being careful to see that he can never manoeuvre you into a position which gives him at least some clear air, either by leaving you dead ahead of him or

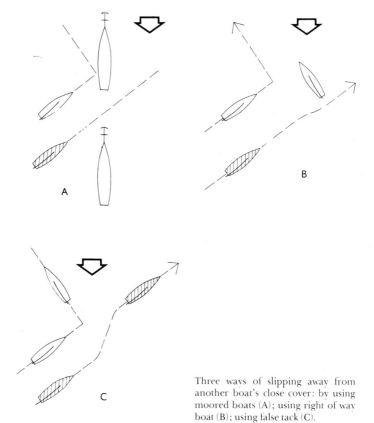

Three ways of slipping away from another boat's close cover: by using moored boats (A); using right of way boat (B); using false tack (C).

slightly back on his weather beam. In close covering you must be careful not to get seduced into being caught by a false tack (he pretends to tack, luffs head to wind with a big flapping of sails and fussing of crew, then falls back onto the old tack again). If the covered boat tries to romp off a little to increase footing speed and try to break clear to leeward, the coverer must also bear off a subtle amount to increase his speed too. Close cover is vitally necessary if you have broken ahead by virtue of downwind speed but know full well that the boat you are trying to hold back is faster upwind than yours.

The lee bow cover

Remember that, when covering, the lee bow position is in many ways safer and more aggressive than the weather bow position, for the reason that backwind from the sails on the lee bow will radiate and eddy in the boat's wake while the simple wind shadow will only be as wide as the covering boat's sail plan. The weakness of the lee bow position is that if you are not laying a mark or the finish and the boat covered splits tacks, the coverer cannot immediately respond unless he wants to be lee-bowed by the boat he was just covering. A common beginners' fault is to try to cover too late, to find the enemy has been able to slip away through their lee. If in doubt one can always tack dead ahead. The backwind effect will soon cause the covered boat to sag down to leeward of you.

How close to another boat can you tack? The answer is to be found in the Definitions of the Racing Rules and, I can tell you, is close indeed. The point is that the boat tacking has to keep clear of others on a tack, but according to the definitions, the tacking manoeuvre is completed – and hence a new tack started – as soon as the tacker has borne away 'to a closehauled course'. It is not necessary to gather full speed, or to be heeled and the crew sitting out, or even for the sails to be fully sheeted home. All that is required is that the bow should be pointed roughly 45 degrees off the wind.

In practice this means that the boat behind will often have to alter course to avoid running into the stern of the boat which

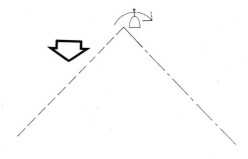

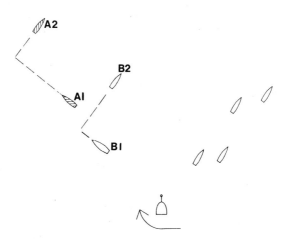

Herding: on the last windward leg of a race, if you have established a narrow lead over several boats, you can sometimes defend your lead more effectively by herding them together so you can stay between the whole group and the mark. This is done by immediately applying close cover and taking the wind of any boat that shows signs of leaving the group and taking a flier (B1). Immediately he goes onto port tack, rejoining the herd, only loose cover is applied (B2). If he tries to break away by tacking, close cover is again immediately applied.

has just tacked ahead of him. You might say that with this
definition Tacking has become a means of Attack.

Approaching the finish

As you approach the finish line, you must devote more and
more of your thinking to planning your finish. As a racing
reporter I have seen many races thrown away by brilliant
helmsmen finishing carelessly. The reasons for this are
obvious. First, in the region of finishing lines of important
races crews are both tired and excited; secondly, one finds such
a confusion of spectator boats, large and small, belching hot
exhaust gases which burn up the wind, or sailing around with
sails which simply blanket the wind, that the wind almost
ceases to exist near the finishing line.

The best end

Hardly any finishing lines are laid exactly at right angles to the
wind direction and exactly upwind of the last mark. Every line
which is not so laid – and this is a large majority of finishing
lines – will have a favoured end for finishing and an ill
favoured or more distant end. If one was simply finishing by

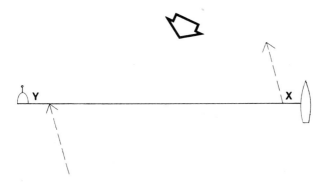

Finishing: if neither the line nor the wind changes, the best end of the line for
finishing is the opposite end to the best starting point. Here, as it was best to
start at X, it is best to finish at Y.

165

approaching the same starting line from which one had departed (and sailing of course in the same direction), one could simply say that the best end for starting is going to be the worst end for finishing. But the Olympic course lays its finish abreast the weather mark and not at the lee mark where the start was. So usually in modern races the two lines, start and finish, bear no relationship.

Of course from the air, or even from the upper deck of a sizeable spectator or committee boat, it would be quite easy to spot which is the nearer end. But approaching the line as the racing crew does while leaning out or lying along decks only a few feet above the waves, it is difficult indeed to spot how the

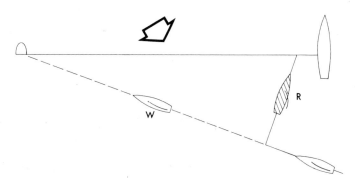

The finishing line: always tack towards the end of the line you can lay soonest. Boat W is wrong, boat R is right.

line lies. One guide, although by then it is often too late, is that assuming you are sailing on a tack which will just clear one end, there will come a time when by tacking you could lay the other end. As this crucial tacking point approaches you should be able to estimate which tack will take you across more quickly, i.e. which tack will be shorter – the one you are now sailing on or the other. If it is the other remember the time it will take to tack and regain speed. This will have to be added to the length of that tack to the finish.

Finishing lines are commonly much shorter than starting lines. This has the effect of herding everybody more closely together and making finishes much closer than you would expect. Because of this, tactical foresight is essential if you are not to be caught at a disadvantage, and I refer to being caught on another's lee bow when neither of you can lay the line. He will be able to sail on until he is absolutely sure of laying when he tacks. By this time you will have overstood so that when you

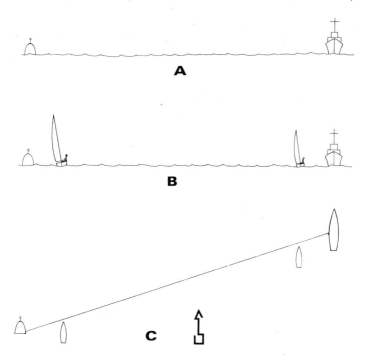

A

B

C

Assessing the line: from sea level it is usually very difficult to gauge which end of the line is closer, particularly if, as is usual, one end is marked by a buoy and the other by the much larger shape of a committee vessel. Stand up to get a higher view. Often you can use other objects of known size, such as other boats finishing or nearby spectator boats to help you make an accurate assessment. In A it is almost impossible to tell the nearer end, but if two boats have received guns close together in B, you can tell the line is as in C and the port end is nearer.

put about, the moment he puts about, you will tend to fall back on his weather quarter. (You could not tack before he tacked because you would have put your boat under his bows). Often it will pay, even when on starboard tack, to up helm and sail under the stern of another, if by this means you are sailing towards the line while he is sailing along it. You always want to be on the finishing tack which cuts the line at the widest angle, ideally at right angles. It is no good being on a tack which hardly converges. It will feel like a lifetime as you sail on and on, hardly closing at all with the finish.

The nearness of a finishing line is often difficult to judge because you may not know the size of the marker buoys. They are often much bigger than they seem to be. You may see what

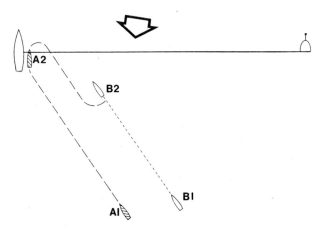

Race right to the finish: you in boat A cannot quite lay the finishing line, and because the committee boat is a mark of the course you cannot hail B about – if you do you must retire. But since only part of the boat need cross the finishing line, you can save your race by a last-minute luff which just pokes your bow over ahead of B. You remain amenable to the rules until you have cleared the line so you must keep clear of B until he has finished too and go under his stern.

looks like a football and, thinking it to be football size, think it is only 15 yards away. But it is much more likely, nowadays, to be a specially constructed inflatable marker buoy fully 6 feet in height, in which case, for the same apparent size on the water, it will be some 100 yards away. At the other end of the line will be a committee boat, whose features and people should help you establish its scale and hence distance with some accuracy.

If the committee boat is large, do what you can to steer well clear of it. It may very well cast a big wind shadow in its lee.

168

And make quite clear that you know what part of it, whether foremast, mizzen mast or specially erected pole, marks the precise finish.

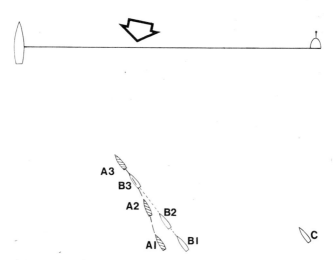

Don't be pipped at the post: boat B is so close on your weather quarter you will not be able to luff and tack as you reach the line, yet as he is going he will lay the line. You must, *in good time,* start to edge out on him, even sacrificing a bit of lead to do so, until you are lee-bowing him, when he will be compelled either to tack to clear his wind, or drop back so that you will have room to tack onto port when you need it. Watch out for other boats in the general area of C who are likely to steal a march on both of you.

Finishing

Remember that you stay amenable to the rules, and hence liable to disqualification for a foul and protest, until your boat has drawn quite clear of the line. You do not have to sail clear across. You can place your bow across and then drop back or you can continue to sail across till your stern has cleared. Once clear your race has finished and you can drift onto the outer limit mark and run into another boat with impunity. But remember that it is good manners to sail well away from the line immediately, so that you harrass neither those finishing behind you nor the race officers as they attempt to take finishing times and identify sail numbers. One of the neatest finishes I have ever witnessed was in the 1968 Olympics at Acapulco, in the Star class. The great Paul Elvstrom was not quite laying the outer limit but he still slanted the slim bow of his boat across the line, took his gun and then deftly threw about onto the other tack, inches before he would have

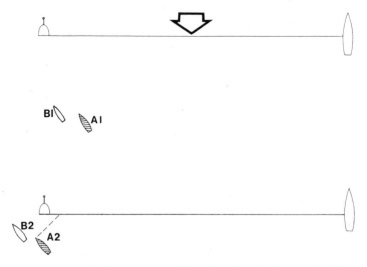

A trap to avoid: don't ever get yourself into B's position. He has a tiny lead, but has allowed A onto his weather quarter and cannot tack until A allows. A of course overstands to a position where he can make the line before B, who has to sail back around the limit mark.

clobbered the mark. The significance of this finish only became clear later. By it, Elvstrom beat the Italian who was in the act of finishing at the other end of the line. This meant that his fellow Scandinavian, Peder Lunde of Norway, had beaten the Italian on overall points and moved up into second place for the Silver Medal. Elvstrom himself was only fourth, the first time he had missed a gold medal in five attempts.

10 Spinnakers

The spinnaker has become such an important part of modern yacht racing that it deserves at least one chapter of its own. In fact I am working on a complete book on the spinnaker.

Spinnakers have always had a love-hate relationship with sailors. When drawing and setting well they can add immensely to the exhilaration and excitement of moving fast, but getting them up and dragging them down afterwards, and keeping them content and quiet in between, is another story. How often they run amok, go berserk, perform the most unbelievable contortions that could never be repeated and which one can hardly describe.

I once pulled up a spinnaker through the centreboard trunk of an International 14. One corner was still attached to part of the spinnaker pole. I have seen the mast of one yacht lassoo the spinnaker of another and make off with it. Matters were not helped when the kidnapped crew let go the spinnaker halyard and it caught aloft, after letting the spinnaker fly yards ahead. Yachts quite commonly sail over their spinnakers, wrapping themselves up as if towelling down after a bath. Spinnakers also have a nasty habit of blowing back behind a boat, then dropping into the sea and transmuting themselves into vast and immoveable trawls fully capable, though made of tissue-thin fabric, of bringing a 20 tonner to a standstill with a jerk.

And all those rollings and broachings that spinnakers have caused – those heart-in-mouth, heart-stopping, stuttering, quite insensate boat stampedes – have made a lot of people frightened of what might happen when the deck becomes a cliff and the rudder entirely ornamental.

The cause of all the troubles that spinnakers are heir to is the very size of these sails, plus their extreme fullness and the fact that they are held and controlled at three corners only. Nowadays a spinnaker may have ten times the cloth area of the mainsail it partners, yet a main is fully controlled along two of its three edges. On a spinnaker all the strains are taken by the corners, while the length of the edges is much shorter than the true girth of the sail. Thus once it turns inside out, or begins to flog or goes up twisted, it becomes difficult to manage and demands, above all, experience and coolness.

Let us dig quickly into the history of this sail. It is closely related to the stunsails (studding sails) once set by square riggers on extra, light spars outboard of their normal square sails when running before light winds. It also has something in common with the raffee set above square sails in these conditions.

The first spinnaker

Every racing skipper knew that a yacht could be made to carry much more sail when scudding downwind than when beating up: the problem was to find a place for it. Some boats carried square sails hung below the main boom and often trailing in the water – hence the term 'water sails'. It was quite a common practice to goosewing jibs by making them fill on the side opposite to the main, and goosewinging could be helped by the use of extemporary booming-out poles. But then somebody thought what a good idea it would be to arrange for a special sail and boom which would be run up when squared away on the weather side. The idea seems to have started in the Solent. It is generally accepted that the yacht *Sphinx* set such a large sail of this type that the Cowes locals nicknamed it '*Sphinx*'s acre', and in the Isle of Wight dialect, very similar to that of Hampshire and Dorset and still extant, it would not take long for those two words to come together to become first 'sphinxer' and then 'spinnaker' (the 'spanker', set as a fore and aft sail by square riggers, is something else again). For the record, *Sphinx* was a cutter of 47 tons owned by Herbert Maudslay, and the new sail was first hoisted at a Royal Yacht Squadron regatta in 1866. Before then most well equipped yachts had hoisted square sails for downwind sailing.

The first spinnakers were quite as flat as the balloon jibs of that time and had hardly more sail area. The spinnaker booms were long and the sail was always set entirely to windward.

It wasn't until 1927, when Sven Salen (inventor of the genoa jib) took his 6 metre *Maybe* to the USA, that the so-called parachute spinnaker appeared. This was such a large sail that it was set around the forestay with its weather edge (luff) set from a pole to windward in the old way, but its lee edge (leach) sheeted to the lee rail of the boat like a jib. The Americans caught on to this advance very quickly and may be said to have led spinnaker development and usage. The old type flat sail is still seen on some old classes such as the British X and other local one-designs. In fact the Flying Dutchman class had been going for several years before some Europeans began taking the lee sheet around and to leeward of the forestay.

All present day spinnakers, with the sole exception of the assymetrical (and highly efficient) 'extras' set by the skiffs of New Zealand and Australia, are of the parachute style and are symmetrical about their vertical axis so that they can be reversed or set back to front and easily gybed.

Closer to the wind

As spinnaker experience and daring has advanced, crews have learned how to carry these sails closer and closer to the wind. On modern offshore yachts, where masthead rig is universal and spinnakers much larger than the rest of sail area put together, it is now usual to hoist spinnakers whenever the yacht is not actually closehauled (in this respect, the British star cut reaching spinnakers of Bruce Banks have made it possible to sail far higher than ever before and have been widely copied). Only in fresh breezes is it impossible to set a modern spinnaker until the wind is aft of the beam.

Up until the second world war the spinnaker was always thought of as a wind-catching bag. This is why Ratsey and other leading sailmakers of the thirties made a practice of putting sizeable holes in the sails, so that the accumulated air could slowly escape and so stabilize the sail.

After the war the Americans, possibly led by Wally Ross of Hard Sails, were the first to realise that most of the time the spinnaker behaved just like the mainsail and jib, and worked best when the wind flowed horizontally across the surface from one side to the other. Once this was discovered it became obvious that spinnakers could be too full for their own good, and the old idea of making parachute spinnakers in two mirror halves joined along the vertical centre seam lost ground.

Today nearly all spinnakers have horizontal seaming and only in the largest sizes do they have vertical seams from top to bottom. Sailmakers have their own ideas about how to shape the upper portions. Even a one design class such as the Soling permits a large and a small spinnaker to be carried in a race, the idea being that a smaller, flatter cut sail will be used for reaching and the larger, fuller sail for dead runs. In fact most leading skippers are beginning to realise that the best reaching spinnaker often makes the best running sail. The Americans taught the British in a couple of America's Cup defeats (*Columbia* over *Sceptre,* and *Constellation* over *Sovereign*) that spinnakers could easily be too big.

No hard curves

Now the aim is to combine flatness with overall extended size. A good spinnaker should have no hard curves anywhere. From any angle it should look as if it is part of the shell of a complete globe (perhaps only a quarter of the surface area of that globe). It should be set so that it reaches out well ahead of the boat, while to leeward it leaves a big gap or slot ahead of the jib and main. In this way the jib and mainsail are allowed to continue doing their own work.

Small differences of cut make large differences to the pulling power and effectiveness of a spinnaker, and some sailmakers, through hard work, constant experiment and careful change have justifiably built up great international reputations for their spinnakers. It does look as if something like finality is being achieved in spinnaker development. Only rule changes will necessitate further marked development.

Control systems

As I suggested at the start of this chapter, the problem is not so much the sail itself as how to set and control it and prevent it

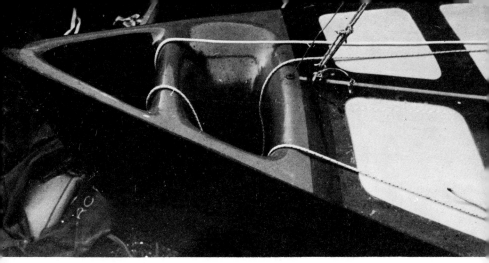

Flying Dutchmen, the fastest two-man centreboard boats, get more and more complicated. This detail of *The Gagman's Boat*, owned and sailed by the French Pajot brothers (1972 Olympic silver medallists), shows their double spinnaker launching chutes. This arrangement calls for two sets of spinnaker sheets and two spinnaker halyards. White patches further aft are plastic sheeting which replaced conventional plywood in the constant search for extra lightness. This was later ruled illegal by the measurers.

becoming your master. Different classes and types of boat, with their different crew numbers and amenities, have led to quite different spinnaker control systems being invented, but there are a few principles which apply universally.

The sail needs to be controlled in some way as it is hoisted. Today this is most commonly achieved by hoisting the sail out of some kind of container. Large spinnakers are still occasionally hoisted in stops, i.e. flaked into a tall, thin vertical sausage and seized with frail cotton thread at intervals of a foot or so, so that when the sail is in position it may be broken out by pulling on guy and sheet. In most craft the spinnaker is hoisted to leeward, where it is safely in the wind shadow of the jib and mainsail. In some two-man racing dinghies it is still normal to lower to windward, after it has been well muzzled. But in most modern dinghies the spinnaker chute is now universal and we will talk about this in a moment.

Pole control

The modern spinnaker is gybed by taking the spinnaker pole from one clew or lower corner and placing it in the other. This

175

is achieved in many ways depending on boat type, but it should be possible, except in two-man boats, to gybe without letting the sail deflate. Poles are normally controlled by uphaul and downhaul lines, the downhauls often being called foreguys and the uphauls, lifts.

If the spinnaker can be hoisted from ahead of the forestay there is a much better chance of it setting quickly and untwisted. This is the principle behind the dinghy chute and also the spinnaker turtle (or bag) used by Dragons and many offshore handicap racers. Some classes, such as the Soling and 5·5 metre, find it is better to hoist from the lee rigging or out of the lee side of the cockpit, but the sail still normally emerges from a stowage bag of some kind.

A practice which has spread from the USA makes for simplification in some respects and difficulties in others. It is to run the spinnaker sheets (the weather one is strictly called a guy and only the lee one a sheet) through the pole end instead of securing the sail corner rigidly to the pole end. This enables the pole to be fixed in position and roughly adjusted before the spinnaker is run up; it also permits the use of the chute and the bag in the lee rigging. The difficulty is that unless the weather sheet (the guy) is pulled around smartly to the pole end, the spinnaker will fill while it is behind the mainsail and on the beam, where it will flog, cause drag and slow and heel the boat.

When lowering using the sheet running through the pole end system, it is possible to leave the pole *in situ* until after the spinnaker is stowed. Thus one can leave the spinnaker drop until later, after one has rounded the lee mark and is again hard on the wind. But this will not be a practical advantage in two-man trapeze boats, where the forward hand will need to get all the spinnaker gear stowed before the mark so that his hands are free for trapezing once the boat is hard on the wind again.

Gybing

Again, depending on the size of crew and the available deck space, various systems have been devised for gybing spinnakers. There are really two kinds of gybe. The first is the

176

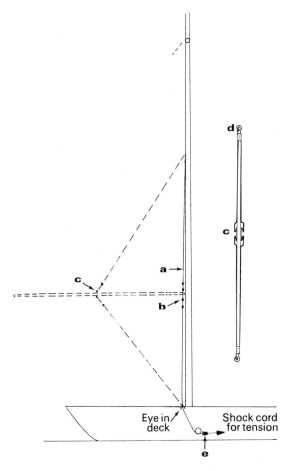

Eye in
deck

Shock cord
for tension

Spinnaker pole lift and downhaul: for a small keelboat or dinghy a combined
spinnaker pole topping lift and downhaul is best. The top is attached to the
mast halfway between the pole attachment and the spinnaker halyard sheave.
The pole is fitted with twin inward-facing cleats (c) which must be carefully
sited exactly at the middle, and click-on end fittings (d) of whatever type you
prefer, but capable of operation with one hand. Knots (b) are placed to support
the pole at whatever level is chosen for conditions. The lower end of the line is
taken through an eye in the deck immediately forward of the mast, round a
sheave and aft to a long length of shock cord to keep it taut when not in use. A
stopper (e) is fitted to take the load on the downhaul, and must be carefully
positioned.

square run gybe where the boat makes only a small change of course. This is the sort of gybe necessary half way along the square run leg when you are tacking downwind, or the wind has shifted slightly. This is a comparatively simple gybe, and providing the spinnaker is kept full, the ultimate speed in getting the pole from one side to the other is not so important.

The other gybe is the reach to reach, often called a 'gold cup' gybe. This is the gybe necessary at the second mark of the Olympic course, the mark between the two reaching legs. This gybe is much more difficult because it means that the spinnaker has to be readjusted through a much wider arc. It calls for more crew co-operation and understanding and more agility on the foredeck. And since, while reaching, the pole exerts a strong push against the mast, it will be more difficult to get the pole transferred from side to side.

Two-pole gybe

Because of this, British and other offshore yachts normally gybe using two poles. This system entails great complication, but it is safe. Each pole needs its own attachment (which also normally runs in its own track) on the mast. Each pole needs its own uphaul and downhaul lines. And instead of single lines to each clew of the spinnaker there must be two, one of which is usually a wire and the other a rope.

The principle of the two pole gybe is that the old pole will be gradually relieved of its duties while the new one is taking over. The new pole is first rigged into position, hoisted up its track on the mast and guyed up and down. But before it is pushed out, the loose, disused, sheet of the pair at the leeward clew is run through its outer end.

Once it is in position the weight is taken on the loose sheet at the other side of the spinnaker. At the same time the loose sheet through the new pole end is tightened until it begins to take the strain. Now the sheet which was taking the strain originally, through the old pole, is slackened. This enables the old pole to be lowered on its uphaul until it falls beneath the spinnaker. To gybe, the sail is now hauled around the forestay by sheet adjustment. Meanwhile the main boom is man-handled or allowed to swing across the boat.

As can be seen, this manoeuvre is complicated and requires good teamwork on the part of sheet handlers and the foredeck crew who will be handling the poles. It can also lead to a great deal of knitting around the mast, and if badly done it is all too easy to stick a pole through the skirt of the spinnaker. But it does keep the sail under tight control, so is effective in heavy weather or in the dark.

Dip-pole gybe

The two-pole gybe was developed in 12 Metre America's Cup racing. It was also made obsolete by these same people who hit on the dip-pole gybe which is now favoured by most crack American and Australian offshore crews.

One pole and its gear is used instead of two, but two lines, which become sheets or guys as required, are still needed to each clew of the spinnaker. First the loose sheet on the weather or pole side is tightened and the sheet through the pole end slackened at the same time the pole uphaul is slackened. Then the pole·is swung forward and down towards the stemhead. Your most nimble crewman now goes forward, carrying with him the loose sheet from the other side of the sail. As the pole end comes within reach he unclips from its fitting the old weather sheet (the one which had been doing the work and which will normally be of wire). Once this is out he now swings the nose of the pole under the forestay, over the pulpit and towards the new weather side after gybing. In order to do this there must be no stowed headsails hanked to the forestay and the pulpit will need to be low, the pole comparatively short and its inner end high up the mast. Otherwise it will be necessary to detach the inner end from the mast, which will lose half the benefit of the dip-pole gybe. He snaps into the end fitting the loose sheet from the other side (which will be of wire), taking care to see it is led through the fitting in the right direction. The pole is then hoisted by its uphaul on the new side and also hauled aft into approximate position. At the same time the main boom is gybed.

179

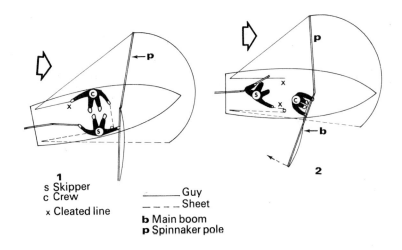

1
s Skipper
c Crew
x Cleated line

_____ Guy
_ _ _ _ Sheet
b Main boom
p Spinnaker pole

2

A splendid refinement on this gybe was practised by at least one 12-metre in the most recent America's Cup series, the object being to dispense entirely with anybody forward of the mast. Slave lines operated from abreast the mast, leading through the spinnaker pole and out at the outer fitting. These were clipped onto the spinnaker sheets and automatically did the work of taking one out and putting the other in. The purpose of this refinement was to remove the weight of crewmen in the bows, where unnecessary weight is always harmful. I believe the fitting which made this possible, the hollow pole end, originally was invented in Britain.

Small-boat gybing

Two-man boats do not have the stability or the deck space for automated gear and this sort of gybing. The forward hand simply manhandles the pole from one side to the other. Usually the mainsail is first gybed across, then the crew takes the pole off its mast fitting, releases it from the old weather sheet, clips it over the new weather sheet, then fastens it to the mast again. Uphaul and downhaul will not need to be touched because with small craft they are led to the centre of the boat, the downhaul led back to the mast. The skipper normally

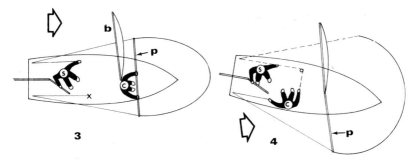

1 Gybing spinnaker in a two-man boat: skipper sits to leeward, holds the tiller and main boom. Crew, to windward, holds spinnaker sheet and has the guy cleated handily at X. In a centreboard boat the board is well up

2 Crew squares spinnaker boom, then gives spinnaker sheet to skipper who cleats it. Skipper ups helm while crew swings boom across. Both skipper and crew are in the centre of the boat and well aft.

3 After the main boom swings across, the crew detaches spinnaker pole from mast, attaching this same end to new spinnaker guy. Skipper corrects helm, counterbalances boat, changes jib sheeting and makes small alterations to cleated spinnaker sheet and guy as necessary.

4 Crew detaches other pole end from the spinnaker and attaches it to the mast. Crew then takes new spinnaker sheet out of cleat, to hold. As crew moves to weather side, skipper moves to lee.

helps out by adjusting the spinnaker sheets (having cleated the main and probably stuck the tiller between his legs).

In most two-man boats the pole is stowed back in the cockpit and completely detached from the uphaul and downhaul, but in recent seasons more and more have experimented with stowing the pole on the foredeck, enabling the uphaul and downhaul to be kept secured. Permanent stowage of the pole on the foredeck, with uphaul and downhaul attached, has become accepted practice in the three-man Soling class, which because it is Olympic, may be assumed to have well developed crew routines. By means of doubled hoisting wires the pole is automatically hoisted parallel to the foredeck, moving up the mast with the equal movement of the outer end (which already holds the weather spinnaker sheet/guy).

The pole is always hoisted before the spinnaker. The foredeck hand will normally hoist the pole first, then the spinnaker. Meanwhile the middle hand will have been busy grabbing the sheets and taking them over winches and adjusting them approximately.

The highest forms of spinnaker handling may be seen in boats of completely opposite types. On the one hand the America's Cup boat, with her eleven man crew and cost-no-object gear, permits sails of well over 2,000 square feet to be thrown about, hoisted and dropped and gybed with hardly a flutter or a falter. On the other one has the Olympic Flying Dutchman class with single, hardworked crewmen producing spinnakers from the bow chutes while already clipped onto their trapeze wires and hanging right out over the weather rail.

Tallboys and sneakers

In small boats the headsail is normally kept set with the spinnaker. If a jib roller furler is fitted, the jib, especially if it is a wide based genoa, will normally be rolled up for a square run, but it should be possible to make it work hard on a reach. On larger craft all manner of special sails have been designed for hoisting in the foretriangle while the spinnaker is up. In the present state of the art, a very tall, narrow 'tallboy' may be tacked to the weather rail, not very far ahead of the mast, for a square run, but will be replaced by a much larger spinnaker staysail (sometimes called a cheater) when the wind draws ahead slightly. Yet I have seen big masthead genoas made to work efficiently under maximum size spinnakers on reaches.

Spinnaker chutes

Now a word about that spinnaker chute or launcher from which small boat crews are able to produce spinnakers like rabbits out of a hat. First, there is a confusion in nomenclature which must be disposed of. Americans and others commonly call their spinnakers 'chutes', which is an abbreviation of 'parachute spinnaker', but since all modern spinnakers are of the parachute type the defining adjective is unnecessary and we would be better advised, if we find the word 'spinnaker' too long, to copy the French and call them 'spis' instead. This would prevent confusion with the new spinnaker chute which is indeed a chute as defined by the dictionary as a 'sloping channel or slide for conveying things to lower level'.

Though David Thomas, British sailmaker, lays claim to having invented this kind of chute, it apparently became commonly used first on the American continent and in the Flying Dutchman class. The idea is simple: forward of the forestay a smoothly rounded mouth, usually fashioned of thin

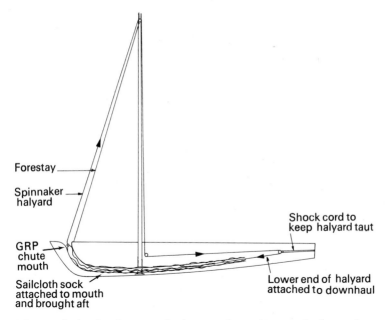

Forestay

Spinnaker halyard

Shock cord to keep halyard taut

GRP chute mouth

Sailcloth sock attached to mouth and brought aft

Lower end of halyard attached to downhaul

Layout of spinnaker chute gear: the chute mouth must be a completely smooth funnel fitted in the deck ahead of the forestay, with no projections of any kind on which the sail can snag going up or down. The sail is stowed in the long sock, which is made of sailcloth but porous or ventilated to let water or air trapped in the sail escape. This is attached, smoothly and without any snag, to the chute, and its length disposed tautly in the boat. The halyard is attached to the head of the sail, taken to its hoisting sheave, down to the heel of the mast (usually internally, but shown here externally for clarity), aft to a block which can be fastened with shock cord to keep the whole system under tension, and then through a hole in the aft end of the sock to the attachment point on the front side of the sail, where there should be a reinforced patch. The halyard needs to be one long length free of knots or fastenings to allow it to run easily, but carefully arranged.

fibreglass, is formed in the triangle of foredeck immediately aft of the stemhead. This tubular, tapering, mouth is led aft under the deck to one side or other of the forestay. Where it becomes circular in section a long sausage or tube of sailcloth is attached to it. This must be half as long as the height of the spinnaker and led aft towards the cockpit of the boat.

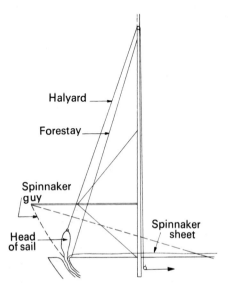

Hoisting from a chute: crew fits the outer end of the pole over the guy, and then fits the pole in place on the mast, set up correctly on lift; the skipper hoists briskly and the spinnaker goes up out of the chute; crew hauls in the guy and adjusts sheet.

At the centre of the spinnaker (by which I mean the halfway point between the two clews and the head, which is not the same as the halfway point between the head and the centre of the bottom edge) is attached the lower end or fall of the spinnaker halyard, but first this end has been led forward through the aforementioned sailcloth sausage and out through the mouth of the chute. The hoisting end of the halyard is attached to the spinnaker head in the normal way. Sheets are kept permanently rove to each clew of the sail.

The spinnaker is hoisted in the normal way. It emerges, head

184

first, from the mouth of the chute. It has to be pulled up quickly to make sure that it doesn't fall over the bow and into the water and get run down. Usually the pole will already have been clipped over the weather sheet. In a two-man boat the skipper will hoist the sail from aft while the forward hand fixes

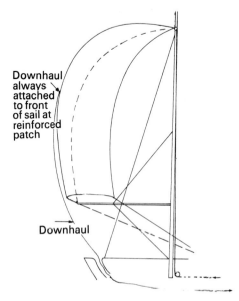

Lowering with a chute: note that the sail downhaul must be set absolutely central on the spinnaker and on the forward side. To lower, the skipper first tightens the downhaul, then uncleats the halyard and hauls quickly on the downhaul, and the sail dives down the chute like a rabbit down a hole. Only after the sail is fully stowed within the chute does the crew unship the pole, because it helps to hold the sail out of the water during lowering.

the pole to the mast, then jumps for the weather sheet (guy), which he secures, and then for the lee sheet, which he will hold.

On lowering, the sail is literally hauled downwards by the other end of the halyard, being pulled aft through the mouth of the chute centre first. The spinnaker will be drawn irrevocably into the maw of the chute, being stowed centre first and corners last. And that is all there is to it. With the system it is possible for a crewman to stay on his trapeze wire even

185

while his skipper is lowering the sail. Hoisting and dropping is much quicker and neater and twists should become crises of the past. The whole process is shown on pages 188–197.

It is much easier to fit a chute in a boat whose bow extends well beyond the jib tack (e.g. FD or Dragon) than in a short-bowed boat such as the International 14 or 505. Nevertheless these latter classes have both found it worthwhile to modify their entire rigs, bringing jib tack, mast and even centreboard further aft, to make room for the prized chutes, which have to be ingeniously squeezed in.

Some one design classes such as the Tempest, and at one time the Fireball, banned holes through their foredecks which ruled out conventional chutes. So owners dreamed up above-deck chutes, with the sail pulled into roller contraptions and stowed close along the deck.

There is no doubt that the chute marks a great step forward in spinnaker handling since it makes the whole thing more automatic and foolproof. But keelboat owners should pause before they copy the dinghy boys. It is not always good policy or even safe to carve a big hole in your boat at its extreme bow. The few Dragons which have fitted chutes have found that they can become boat sinkers if they are not very careful. Some have fitted sliding hatches and other refinements, but at the pre-Olympic regatta at Kiel in 1971 the Dragons with chutes sealed them up altogether.

Cut and material

Returning to spinnaker cut and fabrics for a moment, it seems that much more development is needed in the manufacture of lightweight, stretch free resilient spinnaker cloths. At present far too many stretch out of shape too quickly. Nylon is still the popular material, but one looks forward to something else with even better recovery properties and far less initial stretch. Most spinnaker material is of the 'Ripstop' type, featuring stronger cross threads spaced at about quarter inch intervals and aimed at preventing continuing rips or ladders. But spinnakers are still far too vulnerable to the untaped split pin, the proud screwhead and even the long fingernail.

186

Choice of spinnaker

As I suggested earlier, there is a trend in small day racing boats, away from carrying two spinnakers, one for reaching and one for running, and more in favour of one good, maximum size, all-round sail. But in handicap cruiser racing at least three spinnakers are considered necessary for the well equipped boat. There must be one maximum size, lightweight sail, one so-called storm spinnaker of much smaller size and much heavier material, and there ought to be one extra flat cut, close-reaching sail as big as it is possible to set on a close reach. As a refinement, one should add a light-air ghoster of extremely light cloth and usually of less than maximum area. It might be a good thing for yacht racing – but a bad thing for sailmakers – if stricter limits were imposed on the number of spinnakers that may be carried in any race. I cannot understand why a one-design such as the Soling should permit two different sized sails. One admires the initiative of the Flying Dutchman class in pressing for stricter limits. It is nothing for an offshore owner to blow out three spinnakers, which may easily total £2,000, in a single long event such as the 600 mile Fastnet Race.

As to the many and various systems for setting these sails, you may rest assured that the best system has yet to be discovered. Thinking of new systems is a lot more difficult than playing chess. The snag is that any change is likely to have wide ramifications. Thus if you decide to keep your pole on the foredeck, you will have to forego, in the Soling class, the chance of using a self-tacking jib. In any other boat you will be faced with the fact that the jib sheets will have to be always over the pole and thus they will need to be longer, which might delay tacking. You will need to find a way of clipping the loose downhaul close to the mast so that it doesn't interfere with tacking. Unless the downhaul leads to the centre of the foredeck directly under its attachment point on the pole, you will have to fit some means of locating the forward end of the pole when it is lowered . . . and so on and so on. This is why keen skippers are forever changing, not one thing but all manner of things at once. It also explains why even small racing boats demand so much time from their crews, even on land.

187

This series of photos by John Hopwood, specially demonstrated by Colin Taylor and his wife Cynthia in their Fireball *Utoo,* shows how effective the spinnaker chute can be.

On the words 'Spinnaker up' the crew rigs the spinnaker pole. The skipper delays hoisting until the pole is almost set.

Skipper hauls on halyard, crew at the same time pulls on sheet and guy, which help sail clear the chute mouth.

Sail is now filled with wind by crew's careful adjustment of sheet and guy. The skipper cleats the halyard and steers to help the sail fill.

Spinnaker now set and drawing. Because a chute sets the sail from the bow and ahead of other sails, the spinnaker will usually fill more quickly than if it was hoisted out of the cockpit.

Down spinnaker: note that the spinnaker downhaul line, which should be as light as possible, is always ahead of the sail. The downhaul line is attached to the sail at the intersection of the three lines from the head and the two clews. This ensures that when lowered the three corners of the sail enter the chute mouth at the same time, giving a tidy stow.

Before the skipper releases the halyard he must haul on the downhaul until the latter is tight, then he eases the halyard a little, keeping hold of it with one hand while continuing to haul on the downhaul with the other. Only when he has hauled in about 5 ft of downhaul is it safe to release the halyard entirely. The risk of getting the dropping spinnaker under the bow is more imaginary than real.

The spinnaker pole is kept in place until the spinnaker is almost lowered into its chute. This reduces the chance of the clew getting under the bow.

One of the advantages of the chute system is that when the spinnaker is fully retracted the sheet and guy need little tidying up or overhauling. The pole is still in the set position.

Once the skipper begins to pull in on the downhaul line it is important that he keeps up the pressure so that the spinnaker stows speedily.

Only when the spinnaker is retracted should the crew unrig the pole. It will be found that the spinnaker will stow more easily on a reach than on a dead run, when one flapping clew can block off the chute mouth. The chute is of greatest value in strong winds. In very light airs the downhaul line can be a disadvantage (which is why it should be very light).

John Hopwood

Keep it pulling

How high should you set a spinnaker? The answer is, higher than you would think. The newer, flatter type in particular need to be set high so that their vertical edges can curve away from the rig and increase the slot sizes. The old guide was to try to match the height of the pole corner to that of the free flying corner. Nowadays it is probably better to raise the pole a little more than this. Only in light airs and on square runs should the pole and hence the sail be lowered.

It is almost always better not to hoist the spinnaker chock-a-block to the halyard sheave. Leave a gap of about 18 inches on a boat the size of a 22 foot Tempest. This again increases the slot to leeward. Only hoist all the way if the boat is rolling badly.

When a spinnaker collapses while reaching with a large jib set beneath it, you will get it going again quicker if you first release the jib sheet so that the sail flaps harmlessly. Remember that it is the more important sail, in this case the spinnaker, that has priority.

One exception to the 'high set' rule is the Bruce Banks type of Star cut spinnaker, which on a close fetch is best set with the pole down to the pulpit and the sheet lead like that of a genoa jib.

Set of the pole

In theory, spinnaker poles should always be set at right angles to the mast. This way they will extend furthest away from the mast. In practice it usually pays to angle the pole slightly upwards to relieve some of the strain on the pole uphaul. On a close reach the compression of the pole and the downwards strain imposed by the weather sheet (guy) is enormous, and by cocking the pole so that it lines up with the lead of the weather sheet from the pole down to the weather rail, you will be relieving the pole of these strains. For very close reaches handicap yachts use short, stout jockey poles rigged out from the mast at right angles, to increase the angle of the weather sheet and make it more easily tightened.

198

Trapeze boats will need a lead for the weather sheet somewhere near the weather shroud, under which the sheet may be led when reaching. This will enable the crew to get out on his wire, over the sheet. Otherwise it will cut across his trapeze wire and hamper movement. Such a lead may be a simple hook.

Sheet leads

In theory it is best to have the spinnaker sheet leads as far aft as possible in the boat, right on the transom or counter corners. This will improve the lead angle of the free-flying corner of the sail. In practice though, such a sheet lead position calls for extremely long and stretchy sheets, and a foul at the lead block is difficult to clear. So most people compromise and fit the lead about halfway between the cockpit ending and the stern.

It is normal in two-man small boats to have a single, continuous spinnaker sheet running from one clew of the sail to the other and across the middle of the boat where it is within easy reach of both skipper and forward hand. Knot the sheet to the sail so that in the unlikely event of a foul-up it may be quickly detached. Metal hanks and snap hooks on the clews are too heavy for light weather. Always have a special light-weather sheet.

When hoisting or lowering a spinnaker on any yacht of over 20 feet waterline, be very careful to keep the halyard on a winch all the time. I have seen dreadful cases of burned hands caused by bravery in the face of a half hoisted or lowered spinnaker that filled when it shouldn't. If you have a couple of turns on a winch drum, or even a single turn, you should, in a crisis, be able to throw on another turn which will cause enough friction to let you throw on another and then you will have the halyard locked and safe.

The secret in lowering a big spinnaker is to release the weather corner so that the sail blows to leeward where it will flutter harmlessly because it is attached at only two of its corners. If it remains attached at all three it can bag out and grab plenty of wind or even more water if it dips too low. But if it dips into the water with only one clew attached it should run alongside harmlessly.

199

Never cut a spinnaker halyard however critical the situation. An American crew member in the 5.5 Metre class did this at the Olympics in Melbourne in 1956. The tension came off the halyard so quickly and it ran through its blocks so violently that the strands unwound and frayed out like a released spring, and promptly jammed solid in the sheave at the masthead.

Spinnaker nets

Yachts, especially those with masthead rigs, must guard against the real risk of the spinnaker wrapping around the forestay when square running and rolling in a seaway. One quick safeguard is to keep a jib set on the forestay. The more professional precaution is to rig an anti-wrapping net, which is in effect a skeletal open-mesh jib which doesn't catch wind yet fills in the foretriangle space.

Do not have too heavy a cloth for your heavy weather spinnaker, or you will be tempted to keep it up in too much wind, and it may pull your stick out or roll you under. Better to have the sail blow out!

11 **Tuning**

Tuning is the art and occasionally the science of making the most of your boat. Its importance in the context of winning races can be seen from witnessing comparative performances in a one design class. The well tuned boat can often beat the badly tuned boat by a much wider margin than is found when boats from different classes race together. This can be seen with Solings and Tempests, Flying Dutchmen and 505s.

The relative importance of tuning tends to increase with the size of boat. In a small dinghy the people are paramount. In a 40 foot yacht the design may be paramount but the tuning is easily able to outweigh even that. This chapter amplifies what was said in Chapter 2 about design aspects, and shows how design features built into a boat can be tuned to best effect.

Tuning, to my mind, embraces every factor, simple or abstruse, which affects your boat and her chance of winning. If a 12 footer, though she sets beautiful sails most carefully rigged, is forced to retire from a race because an insecurely fastened rudder pintle falls off, that boat is self-evidently badly tuned. If a Soling fails to hold her place towards the end of an Olympic race, when the wind increases and her mainsail begins to flog because it is overful for the rising wind and cannot be modified to cope with the changed conditions, that Soling is beaten through lack of tuning. Tuning is truly preparation, but it is a nicer word and more vivid too, since it conjures up a picture of a skipper twanging a shroud with his fingers and listening to its pitch.

Let us dispose first of those matters of tuning which are straightforward and unarguable and also fairly obvious. They might include: sending to its maker a mainsail that has an unduly tight leech so it may be eased by slightly letting out about six seams in way of the batten pockets; eliminating 'hum' or high pitched vibration in a rudder blade at speed by blunting or rounding its leading edge and cleaning off imperfections in its trailing edge; gaining better control over mainsail luff tension by fitting a masthead halyard lock and so eliminating all halyard stretch, however slight; fitting taut shock cord loops under the toe straps to hold them clear of the floorboards so that, when tacking, one can get the feet under them quickly and surely without having to look down into the boat. These are elementary benefits.

The hull should, as described earlier, be as stiff as can be achieved and it goes without saying that structures should be as light as possible. Even in heavy displacement craft a lighter hull will always be better for racing than a heavier one because it permits more ballast to be put into the keel and hence the ballast ratio and stability will be increased. The only exceptions are the specialised conditions mentioned in Chapter 2.

Weight concentration

Weights should normally be concentrated as centrally and as low as possible. If the rules permit, planking or skinning at bow and stern should be thinner than amidships. Topsides should be thinner than bottom planking; decks should be thinnest of all. Nowadays few keen offshore racing skippers use that part of their boat which is ahead of the mast for anything but sail storage and perhaps washing facilities. Dinghy classes all have minimum weight limits, but if the limit of your class is easily attained why not build the hull considerably under-weight, then bring it back up to the limit with such features as a particularly heavy centreboard trunk, centre thwart or heavy floorboards? I lay claim to having built the world's first fibreglass Finn dinghy. Low down in the hollow glass floors amidships I placed lumps of lead. I should add that it wasn't until considerably later that rules came out expressly outlawing this practice.

With an understanding of the mechanical functions of a boat, you can prune weight with impunity, lavishing it only on areas of high stress. The hull bottom is clearly stressed, parti-cularly forward and under the mast. So are the chainplate anchorages, the join of keel or centreboard to hull, and the areas of rudder attachment. Rudder fittings deserve a chapter to themselves: they are the commonest source of boat retirements. Never penny-pinch or ounce-pinch on these and make sure that they are strongly secured so that they cannot loosen later. The faster the boat the tougher it will be on its rudder fittings. I suggest that rudder hangings should be strong enough to support the entire weight of the boat.

In the cause of weight concentration stow all heavy weights such as anchors, chains, water, fuel, paddles, spinnaker poles and spares as close to the boat's centre of gravity as possible.

Stress points

Some of today's small racing craft are extremely light and thin-skinned. These boats call for care and understanding. It is unwise to butt rigid members such as bulkheads straight against the skin. Cracking will soon result if secondary members such as longitudinal stringers are not interposed. Changes in the thickness of components should always be gradual to help eliminate the same hard spots and lines of stress concentration. This is why circular hatchways, with no corners, are better than square ones, which always show cracks radiating from the corners after very hard driving. The modern hull is usually a stressed skin monocoque, particularly if it is built of plywood, which is still just about the most efficient material for stiffness to weight.

Modern rigs have immensely increased hull stresses. A modern ocean racer with its stout alloy mast and stainless rod rigging is hardly able to resist the strains imposed by a strong crewman mindlessly continuing to tighten his hydraulic back-stay adjuster long after the safety point has been reached. A fibreglass boat will simply give, an alloy hull will probably stretch. Not long ago two new wood planked ocean racers both had to be quickly slipped soon after launching, when they sprang leaks around the mast heel on initial sailing trials. The boat is on a rack, the base of the mast trying to spear through her belly while the forestay, shroud and backstay attachment points are trying to pull up her ends.

Decks stiffen hulls immensely. Open dinghies such as the International 14 can never be as rigid, even though they are already heavier than comparable decked classes.

Smooth, not glossy

I do not have to tell you that the underbodies of hulls and the surfaces of keels, fins, centreboards and rudders must be smooth. But it is still more important that they should be 'fair' (i.e. present no hollows or protrusions or other imperfections) when scrutinized end on, with the eye close to the surface. Nobody has ever proved the scientific need for gloss and shine – on the contrary, most leading skippers like a matt finish. They say that by rubbing down with very smooth wet and dry sandpaper just prior to launching they dull the surface and make it more easily wetted, the water flowing across evenly and not in separate beads as one sees on a new car body in the rain. Eschew wax polishes in your search for more speed. They will only attract dust and grime. Instead get out the wet and dry and using a stiff flat backboard, rub and rub and rub, until all the high points are finally no more.

Special 'high build' paints are now available. These are designed to leave a thick but comparatively soft paint layer which may be speedily rubbed smooth with wet and dry. But make sure that beneath this paint is either hard fibreglass or impermeable paints of polyurethane or similar types, for the high build paints are porous.

It has been found that if underwater surfaces are coated with liquids of the long-chain polymer type (like detergents), the flow of the water past the boat is completely changed. Instead of the normal boundary layer of towed-along water which every hull is doomed to drag with it, the water begins to flow past as if oiled. So impressed were scientists with this phenomenon that they promptly called for the banning of long-chain polymers as underwater coatings or as substances which could be exuded or otherwise introduced to the water around a hull. So you must put them out of your mind even though one or two manufacturers offer special paints claimed to embody their features. Many people wash down their hulls in detergent just before launching, but little can remain by the time the start, let alone the finishing line, is crossed and this practice undoubtedly contributes to pollution.

Yachts which are kept afloat must be given hard antifouling bottom paints. There are paints which incorporate anti-fouling properties but are specially prepared to give surfaces that can be hand rubbed and burnished to produce the desired smooth, matt, fair, racing finish.

Antifouling bags

In many parts of the world keelboats are kept afloat at moorings surrounded by 'boat bags' or boat baths. When the boat returns to her moorings, she is carefully slipped into one end of such a bag. Then the upper side of the bag is drawn up above the water and carefully tied up around the boat until she sits on her own puddle which is sealed inside the bag, cutting her off from the rest of the water. Into this puddle between boat and bag is slipped a special powder or tablets of the sort used by swimming pool owners to prevent the growth of algae (copper sulphate). Used in the boat puddle these chemicals abort algae, blister barnacles, weed-out weed and stymie slime. They do the work of an antifouling paint while permitting the bottom to be given a smoother finish than is usually possible with antifouling. Where slipping is difficult, or limited by cost or club rules, this practice is well known.

As you may have guessed, the only trouble is that the bag is often difficult to manage – and quite impossible in strong currents. It is difficult to fit the boat back into the bag, which may be easily – but always expensively – torn. Bags have been used on 12 Metre yachts.

'Dry sailed' boats

Scientists claim that good GRP only soaks up 1 per cent of its weight and I see no reason to dispute this. Yet keen racing skippers always prefer to keep their craft out of the water between races. In most fibreglass boats there is a large amount of reinforcement which is either hollow or foam-filled fibreglass. There is almost always wood reinforcement and padding too, and of course this increases the soakage potential. But apart from possible soakage and weight gain,

205

the keen racer likes to have his boat where he can get at her, swarm all over her, fondle or scratch her, and generally be in overall command of the situation. It is difficult to check the condition and strength of the gear of a boat afloat – rudder fittings for instance will be under water. So it seems that most small keelboat sailors who can will continue to dry-sail their boats however heavy they may be and however few the cranes to hoist them out.

Underwater shape

The underwater shape of the main hull is something you will be able to do little about. But the fins, boards and rudder and such foils, are another matter altogether. We take the desired shapes very much for granted. Most believe the writers and lecturers who tell them that the best sectional shapes for these foils have a blunt nose, with a parabolic leading edge, maximum width about one-third the distance back, and from there a straight taper to the sharp trailing edge. As to ideal thickness-to-width ratios, there has recently been a feeling that fatter than usual sections have something to commend them and that 10 per cent thickness to width is nothing out of the way. As mentioned earlier, from my own experiments with fat sectional shapes of this classic type I am not convinced that they are the answer. The fact is that in dinghies, thin metal plates with sharp leading and trailing edges have never been proved, beyond all doubt, inferior all round to the thicker, wooden, streamlined boards which in theory should be better. My advice is to make both fins and centreboards on your boats as thin as is possible with regard to the necessary structural strength and stiffness. You may in theory be giving away efficiency upwind but you will be gaining in every other respect. If dealing with a centreboard, its trunk can be narrower and hence there will be less turbulent water being dragged around. If a keelboat, the fin will displace less, will have less frontal area and, providing you don't pinch too much, there is no reason why it should let you down by stalling.

The nose of your fin should indeed be rounded at its

206

extreme point, but beware undue bluntness. George Moffatt, an American one-time dinghy sailor for whom I crewed, and who had done much work on foil shapes and later became world sailplane champion, says that he reckons the best nose should have a radius of about 0.40 per cent of the width of the foil. Thus if your centreplate is 14 inches from leading to trailing edge (pretty typical for a small dinghy) its nose should have a radius of 0.056 inches, which means a semi-circle of hardly more than 0.1 inch across. I value Moffatt's judgement, not only because of all the experimental work he did on his International 14 with his various board and rudder blade shapes and proportions but because his later great success in gliding proves that he must have a sure instinct for the flow of air and liquid over shapes. He says that for boards the NACA 0006 section is about the best. This gives a thickness of 6 per cent of width (what the flyers call 'chord'). He also says that maximum thickness should be 30 per cent back from the leading edge, and stresses the need to make the trailing edge just as sharp as humanly, practically possible, while the taper to it should be straight. Others, such as Tony Marchaj, a leading sailing theoretician and experimenter, say that one can cut off the last 10 per cent of the width of a board with impunity and thus blunt the sharp trailing edge by cutting it off sharp and square.

Rudders

Moffatt says something else that has a bearing on my own experience, though it is not born out by it. He reckons that rudder blades, because they are operating at constantly and often widely changing angles of attack, should have blunter noses than centreboards. When I discovered that a New Zealand Finn skipper who was particularly fast offwind was using a rudder blade which had a cross section with a nose whose radius was precisely half the maximum thickness, I decided that I would get such a rudder blade for my Tempest. This I did, but it did me no good; in fact I believed I was sailing slower. So I gradually started fining down the leading edge of the blade until now it is completely conventional. I decided that if one steers a boat carefully and well, there is no need to change rudder attack angles much more than the keel is changing. And since in a boat such as a Tempest which has a very small keel, the rudder blade must also be pressed in to help reduce leeway, it makes sense that it should be shaped like the centreboard or fin keel.

All this must be very confusing to you. In a way this is my object since your own confusion will now match the actual confusion of many so-called experts on the matter who are not as sure as they pretend to be. If you take my advice, your underwater foils will be as thin as they can be without ever breaking or twisting, have a slightly rounded leading edge, and a nice flat taper to a sharp trailing edge.

Much more important than the precise nature of the cross sectional shape (if the precise shape was critical you can be sure that experts would have found this out years ago) is the fairness of the foil as a whole. Even a slight warp will greatly impair efficiency, for a warp means that part of the foil will be operating at the wrong angle and will be dragged through the water. As soon as a foil warps, throw it away. Be careful to store foils out of the sun and preferably on edge in a controlled climate. Examine them frequently.

Leading edges

Look for imperfections in the leading edge and remedy them immediately. Any projection at the front will lead to swirls of water which can easily build up into vortexes as they spiral back along the board. A rounded leading edge is stronger and more practical in this regard than a sharp one.

It goes without saying that a fin keel must be accurately aligned fore and aft on a yacht and bolted up completely solid. But few centreboards are ever fitted quite as solidly as they should be, and as I said in an earlier chapter, I don't like the board that alters its angle. The centreboard trunk must be locked into the boat rigidly and I think the centreboard must have no more freedom of movement than is necessary to get it up and down. A slippery lining to the inside of the case of some such material as PTFE (Teflon), and rollers in the board itself, can help it to fit well. Neoprene or rubber sealing strips at the bottom of the slot will help to diminish harmful water turbulence inside the slot. Test your board for possible twist. Boards take a much bigger strain than is often realised.

Before buying any centreboarder or fin keeler, whether new or secondhand, check that the centreboard trunk or fin keel is accurately aligned with the centreline. It hardly needs me to tell you that this is probably the most important requirement of all. A check can usually be made with long straight laths being put each side of fin or board.

Rudder hangings take a beating, and the faster the boat the bigger the beating is. They should be designed to resist gradual enlarging of the holes because of the sideways and wracking strains (not to mention the occasional grounding and unavoidable collisions with flotsam). Screw fastening is never good enough: bolts should go through reinforced hull material.

Tillers and their extensions can hardly ever be too long, and are very commonly unnecessarily heavy. There should be a universal joint between tiller and extension and there are today several good standard fittings for this purpose. If you do much winter sailing do not choose an aluminium tiller extension – they can be terribly cold to the touch in December.

The mast

And so to the rig: first the mast. Today 99 per cent of masts are made of aluminium alloy. The quality and properties of this alloy hardly vary from one maker and another. Though in the smaller spar sizes silver spruce might possibly make a better spar because it is lighter, it is so difficult to obtain in the necessary quality today that this wood might just as well be forgotten.

My advice on all masthead rigged boats of the ocean racer type is to concentrate on obtaining as stiff, light and as sectionally small a spar as possible. Do not let it bend and certainly do not *try* to make it bend. But even masthead rigged spars should be tapered, not only at the top but at the foot. Simple mechanics indicates the need for this.

Bending spars

With smaller craft and foretriangles lower than the masthead, some fore and aft bend is nearly always desirable if full advantage is to be taken of full sails for lightish weather and broken water. But here one must utter a warning against extremes. Racing has taught the experienced that too much bend is as harmful as too little. Exaggerated bend is only necessary to make a badly cut mainsail set better.

Controlled bend not only helps flatten a mainsail to cope with rising wind, but for some less determinable reason it helps get a boat through a seaway – the give in the rig acting rather like the suspension in a car to iron out the rough water surface. Undoubtedly the best sailor through a seaway is Paul Elvstrom. He has lived all his life on the bank of a choppy area of water, besides which he is a genius. He has always insisted on surprisingly flexible masts; masts made under his name (made in France) for the FD class are tapered to an extreme thinness transversely in their upper sections, but are kept quite deep fore and aft. The idea here is that only a small amount of mainsail flattening is needed in the powerful, modern FD, but the considerable sideways bend off to leeward of the top helps considerably in getting through a sea quickly, by slackening the leech of the mainsail and in adding twist at the top of the main. Sailors using such masts will not be able to point as high as others with stiffer spars but in sufficient wind and waves they will very likely arrive at the weather mark first faster because of much faster footing. However, they are likely to find themselves at a disadvantage in lighter conditions.

Compromise is the answer in masts as in most other aspects of sailing boats. An over-stiff mast might work fine in light airs and smooth waters and will assuredly let you point high to windward and go fast downwind. But in a fresh breeze it is likely to leave you overpowered when others, with bendier spars, are still able to cope well.

It is generally realised today that one can get away with a lighter, smaller spar if it is cantilevered in the hull, i.e. held securely at both the keel and deck levels. This significantly stiffens the lower part of the spar. The only advantage of a deck stepped mast is that it may be a couple of feet shorter. Yet it will need to be heavier, particularly when account is taken of the weight of the post that is required beneath it. The heel should always be locked tightly into its step fitting in order that twist be eliminated, unless it is intended in the design of the rig. With most modern rigging systems no sideways movement should be permitted at deck level, otherwise the cantilever effect is lost. Fore and aft movement is another story, for by permitting a controlled amount at deck level one can control the entire mast bend. Thus it is that most small racing boats have rams, or levers and wires, to adjust fore and aft mast movement through the deck slot (or mast partners) while underway.

It is only in recent years that mast makers began to realise how savagely they could taper the top of their masts. It was probably the wooden Finn class mast that led the way because skippers tapered these with planes between races. Masts hardly ever break near the top, so it is reasoned that most masts are too big and stiff at the top. The simple mechanical fact is that the strains are much reduced near the extremity. Many advanced masts now have a mast cap section which is actually smaller than the mast groove attached to it.

Mast sections

The argument about whether the ideal mast section is thin walled, large section and light in weight or thick walled, small in section and usually higher in weight, will never be finally resolved. Obviously there must be a compromise here. On the one hand is the need for lightness, on the other the need to promote a clean flow of air over the mainsail and also to reduce parasitic drag. It does look as though early aluminium alloy sparmakers, particularly in England, tended towards too light and too large a sectional shape. At present the unmistakable trend is towards smaller mast sections, which naturally mean thicker walls and a higher overall weight. First signs of this movement probably came from Australia with the de Havilland and Alspar masts which performed so well in Flying Dutchmen.

It ought to be explained that the smaller, thicker-walled

section ends up heavier because of its inherent lack of stiffness. Stiffness increases with the distance of the walls from the centre axis of the section, so to make the smaller, less wind-catching section sufficiently stiff needs more metal, and hence weight, per foot than in bigger sections. The latest sparmaking idea is to extrude small ridges in the external walls of the mast which are supposed to induce small vortexes in the wind flow and prevent the build-up of much bigger turbulence. Treat this as a gimmick until somebody can prove the worth of the idea.

Welding softens the metal and changes the characteristics of the finished mast. This is particularly important at the top of the mast, where taper is normally achieved by cutting out a long narrow vee in the spar and then squeezing the edges together and welding up. It is unusual to treat and harden masts after welding, so any great amount of welding is harmful. For this reason one or two sparmakers now offer extruded, tapered topmasts which don't need welding. A French manufacturer sews up his gussetted mast with fine wire, instead of welding it together.

When you are faced with a choice of mast shapes and makes – as for the FD, 505 or Fireball classes, for instance – my advice is to act with caution and conservatism. Find out first what the top skippers are currently using in the class. Make sure there is no new breakthrough design just around the corner, and treat it with suspicion if there is. Four years after his first Gold Medal, Pattisson was still sticking to the same Alspar mast section, though he changed his boat and every sail in that time. But he did win his second Gold Medal, in 1972, with a French Elvstrom spar.

Rigging

Windage and drag are caused by rigging as well as the mast itself. Aerodynamicists are quick to point out that a wire causes much more resistance than its slim frontal area suggests, and where you have two or more wires close together, or a wire is close to the mast, often the wind decides not to blow between and the effect is that of a solid obstruction. Therefore rigging wires must be reduced to the barest minimum. Nowadays it is common to lead nearly all running rigging inside a mast, out of the wind. As to the standing rigging, more and more in the small classes this is being reduced to an irreducible single forestay (which is often extremely slim, since the wire luff of the jib carries the load) and one shroud each side.

Spreaders

To achieve the lightest, smallest mast, it is necessary to further support the lower part of the mast by spreaders between these shrouds and the mast itself. Enough is now known about these spreaders to be able to say with fair assurance that it is best if they are rigidly fixed to the mast (they used to be allowed to swing freely: later the amount of swing was proscribed but not entirely eliminated). Their length, height and angle are each critical to the bend characteristics the mast will have. If the mast is cantilevered and strongly held at deck level, the spreaders should be considerably higher than the mid-span point between deck and upper shroud attachment (which was the common place for them). Two-thirds of the distance upwards is probably best.

To carry the lightest, smallest mast possible, one has to limit bend. You will not be able to eliminate it entirely, but by trying to limit it, one will, with a small light mast, end up with about the right amount. One best limits the bend by setting the angle of the spreaders so that they distort the natural straight line of the shroud from deck to mast, by forcing the shroud forward (about $1\frac{1}{2}$ inches on a FD). The result is that the tight wire tries to pull the spreader and hence the mast backwards.

In the same way, by shortening the spreaders until they try to pinch the shroud inwards, perhaps an inch, forward bend is further inhibited. Leading sparmakers now provide spreaders whose angle with the mast and length may be quickly and easily adjusted between races.

This fixed spreader rig seems to fit most small boat classes very well. There seems no reason today for having extra diamond wires over straight spreaders, jumper struts above the upper shroud attachment, lower preventer shrouds or other bits and pieces. There are, however one or two special rigs, such as that on the International 14 which has an unusually low foretriangle and long topmast, where extra rigging may be necessary (in this case, the fitting of jumper struts).

The recommended backswept spreader rig needs to be very tight. Normally the jib halyard is used to tension the jib luff and hence the whole rig. The jib luff is sometimes kept tight to windward by the tightness of the mainsheet. It is true to say that the larger and wider-based the jib, the tighter its luff and the entire rig needs to be.

Mast rake

Most top boats in the advanced small boat classes can now adjust shroud tension and jib halyard or forestay length under way. Thus the crews have complete control over mast rake and rig tension. Levers are commonly used on shrouds, being thrown off when the weather mark is rounded. For some not entirely clear reason, most boats go best with their rig well raked to windward and with the masthead well forward downwind. The latter helps downwind steering by lessening the need for rudder. Upwind, most boats seem to go best with a marked aft rake to their masts (this does not apply to the masthead rigged ocean racing type). The need for rake is less marked in light winds. The latest development is towards the use of hydraulics for rig tensioning and adjustment.

Masthead rig

Masthead rigged yachts call for a permanent backstay from masthead to stern. This is the only way of keeping the forestay sufficiently tight. The shrouds are normally led to the deck abreast the mast and pass over quite wide fixed spreaders set at right angles to the centreline. These spreaders should be as long as possible with regard to the ability to sheet the jib hard in when beating to windward. The overlapping genoa jib will reach aft of the spreaders. As people are learning to sail fast

214

with jib leads closer and closer to the centreline, spreaders need to be shorter and shorter (and shroud chainplates further and further inboard). For this reason there is much to be said for having two sets of spreaders one below the other, giving a so-called 'two panel' rig, even in quite small boats of Half Ton and even Quarter Ton Cup size. Masthead rigged boats normally carry double lower shrouds each side, led up to the roots of the lower spreaders and splayed fore and aft on the deck to give the mast fore and aft support. Searching to reduce windage, some designers have dispensed with the forward pair of lower shrouds and replaced them with a single lower forestay which is sometimes given a very powerful bottle screw or hydraulic device. The idea is to use this for inducing a forward bow in the mast, but this is another idea whose benefits nobody has been able to prove to me. The disadvantage of a lower forestay is obvious – it interferes with spinnaker pole handling.

Rod rigging

Rigging needs to be as stretch-free as possible. For this reason single filament rods are really better than laid wires, although they do have the disadvantages of being more liable to damage and to fail suddenly and without warning. The most advanced shrouds of all are given a streamlined or lenticular section, so reducing windage further. Latest thinking points to the fact that high tensile steel stretches less than stainless – but of course it rusts very quickly, and so would need to be replaced frequently.

Booms

There have been fashions for flexible booms, but the fashions have been passing and at the moment most knowledgeable skippers, whether of large or small boats, will recommend stiff booms. To obtain stiffness without much weight, a large-diameter thin-walled section is called for – the reverse of the mast situation. A stiff boom seems to confer better control over the mainsail and mast bend. A bendy boom will only flatten the bottom part of a mainsail and fullness here doesn't matter, even in a hard blow, because this part of the sail area is so low. A large section boom will also help to reduce the pressure losses at the bottom of the mainsail which occur when air flows down from the high pressure to the low pressure side. The large boom helps to make the flow more even and more horizontal over the lower part of the sail, proved by wool tuft flow tests (an end plate effect and a little extra downwind sail area).

Rig position and helm

A great deal of nonsense is heard about the question of fore and aft position of the rig relative to the centre of lateral resistance of the hull. If the rig is too far forward the boat will carry lee helm and will want to bear off all the time, unless forced to do otherwise by constant leeward helm pressure. This makes sailing difficult to say nothing of the inherent danger. But if the rig is too far aft the boat becomes 'hard mouthed'; she forever tries to round up into the wind and strong weather helm is called for to control the tendency. Any undue helm angle slows a boat so one tries to position the rig so that the boat, when heeled a few degrees, sails more or less straight with no rudder necessary.

What is immediately apparent is that a boat with slight weather helm, i.e. with the rig set slightly back, is far easier to sail than the perfectly balanced boat. Slight weather helm creates a helm pressure whereas perfect balance gives a dead, unpositive feeling. All the same, I would dare to state that the perfectly balanced boat is potentially faster. In a hard wind, as heel increases and sail fullness moves aft, you will get your weather helm soon enough. In most fat, modern boats it can never be totally eradicated.

Small fore and aft adjustments to mast position will never make their effect felt, even to the most sensitive helmsman. That is why I say that so much nonsense is talked on the subject. Neither will rake alterations change it much. If you race a 14 foot boat you will need to shift your mast at least 4 inches at a time; if a 40 footer, at least 1 foot. Even then the basic hull and rudder shape will influence helm 'feel' more than anything else.

As a general rule it does seem that most boats can be made to go better by moving their rigs forward. Yet, reasoning that the Tempest mast was heavy and because of the fineness of the hull forward it would promote undue pitching in waves, I once moved mine a full 12 inches back. I went noticeably faster to windward (but not faster than the best boats which had masts perhaps 14 inches further forward than mine) and only began inching it forward again when I became tired of losing place after place offwind (the reason for which might not have been at all related to mast position).

Far better than altering mast position to give a balanced helm is to keep your boat upright.

Sail sheeting

Sheet lead position is possibly the single most important tuning consideration. Just as a powerboat will lose much of its efficiency if its propeller shaft is aligned at an incorrect angle, so sails lose much of their power if the angle at which they are sheeted is incorrect. With sails there is another vital consideration: an incorrectly aligned headsail will not only lose power itself but harm the power of the mainsail set behind it.

Jib and mainsail, and to a lesser extent spinnaker, jib and mainsail, must be considered as single, interdependent entities. It will help if you try to take a bird's eye view of them. Earlier in this book we considered at some length the need to make the slot between the weather side of the jib and the lee side of the mainsail as conducive to smooth and speedy airflow as possible. If this air slot is obstructed or unduly narrowed, or if it turns through too sharp an angle, the flow will be slowed or completely broken down and sailing efficiency vitally harmed. Conversely, if the slot is unduly wide and there is no attempt to funnel and lead the air onto the lee of the main, one will needlessly lose a chance of increasing the main's power output.

Jib angle

The most important aspect of lead position is the lead of the jib sheet. One must decide how far out from the centreline and how far aft of the jib clew to position it. In theory, the nearer to the centreline one can take the lead the higher the boat will be able to point into the wind when closehauled. But this narrow angle will seriously affect the slot, narrowing it. Moving the lead forward has much the same effect since the leech of the jib will be tightened and moved closer to the lee side of the mainsail, unless this too is brought in closer to the centreline.

It should be easy to see that it is safer to have the jib lead too far out and too far aft than otherwise. One may not point quite as high as the optimum but at least the slot will be open and the mainsail unimpeded.

One should realise that the two broadly different sailing boat types need different sheet lead treatment. The powerful, fast type, either multihulls or with crews on trapezes, are able to generate so much resistance to heel that when sailing them to windward it pays to concentrate on speed through the water rather than pointing higher and higher. Therefore, on these types the lead usually cannot be positioned very close to the centreline. Set on a line at 13 degrees to the centreline is usually about the limit.

But with narrow keelboats, which soon run out of stability when upwind and begin to heel excessively unless eased in some way, the considerations are entirely different. Such boats need to be feathered into the wind as close as possible in order to keep on their feet. And it is possible to sail them very high indeed in fresh breezes (unless wave considerations dictate otherwise). On these boats the leads can, with care, be brought extremely close to the centreline perhaps to as little as 7 degrees. If the jib is tall and narrow, as in the Star and to a lesser extent the Soling, the angle can be still narrower than with wide-based jibs such as are used on Dragons and offshore racers.

Here a word of caution must be introduced: the closer to the centreline one carries the jib sheet, the more careful one must be not to overtighten the sheet. All those, such as Paul

Elvstrom, who successfully manage to sheet their Soling jibs very close in, carry a great deal of twist, not only in the jib but in the mainsail too. To some extent jib twist can be incorporated in the sail cut, but care must still be exercised not to overtighten the sheet, while care is even more important with mainsail sheeting.

Recently, in boats with overlapping genoa jibs, such as Dragons, Flying Dutchmen and offshore racers, there has been the same trend towards moving leads closer to the centreline. The winner of the One Ton Cup in 1971 had her sheets closer to the coachroof coaming than to the rail; the same is true of many Dragons. Many FDs now have big holes in their side decks to permit the underdeck lead (common in these boats because of the class rules) to be brought inboard. But I would dare to say that these experiments with genoa jibs have been less than conclusive. As soon as the wind freshens at all, be sure that the skippers of these boats, mindful of the narrow slots, move their leads out towards the rail again.

Always remember that wind strength has a vital bearing on jib lead position. The harder it blows the further out and the further aft the lead will need to be. Nothing is worse than being caught out with the lead too far in and forward. The jib leech will be tightened unduly, the slot will be narrowed, and the mainsail will revolt by backing and flogging just aft of the mast.

There can be no specific rules about jib lead position. You can only arrive at the best position for your sail cut, crew weight and boat type by careful, measured experiment. Start by copying the lead positions of the best boats in your class.

As soon as one is off the wind the jib lead can profitably be taken right out to the rail, and here the beamy boat has an advantage over the narrow one. A special, alternative reaching lead is commonly used. The sheet is speedily moved out to this wider position by means of a Barber hauler. Barber haulers are without doubt worth their weight and complication in boats without spinnakers, but when a spinnaker is carried it is far more important to get this sail up and drawing, than to fiddle around with Barber haulers.

Mainsheet leads

Until 15 years ago, all boats carried their mainsheets at the after end of the main boom, generally led to tracks or horses on the stern. Since then there has been an almost universal swing towards mid-boom sheeting. Two considerations have led to this new fashion: the need to reduce twist in the mainsail and the need to ensure that the mainsail leech is not over-tightened in hard winds.

Twist is reduced with mid-boom sheeting because the main-sheet does a better job of acting as a kicking strap or boom vang when it is moved forward in the boat. It is simply a question of angles and the downward component. The main-sheet track can be wider and the sheet can be led more vertically. This extra athwartships latitude makes more import-ant the work of the mainsheet traveller adjustment. On both my Tempest and Finn I have found that in a variable wind I am adjusting the traveller when sailing to windward quite as often as I am adjusting the sheet itself. In fact in both boats I usually cleat the sheet and concentrate on the traveller, keeping it cleated (because of the heavy strain) but pulling it in whenever the wind eases, and as quickly letting it out in response to heavier flaws. In this way the tight sheet continues to act as a kicking strap and the mainsail is not allowed to twist unduly whenever the boat is overpowered. Using the popular modern backswept spreader rig, the mainsheet is the biggest factor in keeping a tight jib luff, and if one is frequently easing the sheet one is as often allowing the jib luff to sag off.

With the old fashioned mainsheet lead to the boom end there was always a tendency for the boom to bend upwards in the middle when the wind increased. This had the effect of increasing leech tension, which was the reverse of what was needed. With mid-boom sheeting, it is the outer end of the boom which tends to bend upwards, and this eases the leech just when needed.

The one exception to the swing to mid-boom sheeting is to be found in those 'feathering' classes already mentioned, such as the Soling, where jib sheet leads are now carried very close to the centreline. If the jib is not to cause the main to back too much, the main must also be carried very close to the centreline. It is a fact that boom-end sheeting gives more precise control of the lateral positioning of the boom at very close angles and reduces the need to move the traveller to windward of the centreline in very light winds. But this is a specialized business, of little concern to dinghy sailors.

It is my experience that the mainsheet traveller needs to be as close to the boom as possible. This is one reason why booms should be low and the traveller or horse high. If the distance between them is too large one is unable to control precisely the angle of the boom without undue vertical tension, and with modern, powerful sheeting systems it is only too easy to over-tighten mainsheets, which results in over-bent spars and distorted mainsails.

Boom angle

As a general rule the mainsheet traveller will have to be eased off to leeward (and hence the mainsail angle increased) as wind speed increases. This narrows the angle of attack of the sails and reduces heeling forces without bringing the hull so close into the wind that the boat begins to slow unduly and makes overmuch leeway.

Una rigged, single-sail boats can carry their mainsails profitably at wider angles than boats with jibs. Boats with narrow-based jibs can carry their mainsails at wider angles than boats with broad-based genoa jibs. The most useful guide is the amount of backwind in the front of the mainsail. Some backing is almost always present, except with a very flat mainsail, but an excess amount of backing will obviously harm the air flow and will even shake the complete rig and the hull also.

The Cunningham hole

Mention has already been made of the tendency for the fullness or flow in a sail to move aft as wind increases. This is the very reverse of what is required. As jib flow moves aft the slot is choked; as mainsail flow moves aft the mainsail leech is tightened, weather helm is increased and so is heel.

221

To counteract this natural tendency most keen skippers now fit some means of increasing or adjusting the tension on the luffs of their sails. The common way of doing this is by pulling the sail downwards through a reinforced point a few inches above the sail tack. The effect of extra luff tension is to bring back the flow towards the front of the sail again. The downhaul line used to pull down the sail in this way is called a 'Cunningham' line after well-known American skipper and racing driver Briggs Cunningham. The sail eyelet or cringle on which it pulls is called a 'Cunningham hole', and on a mainsail of 20 foot luff length is usually about 8 inches above the tack. The line needs to run over a powerful purchase if sufficent tension is to be induced.

A Cunningham adjustment is often fitted to the tack of a jib for the same reason, but this is obviously very difficult to arrange if a jib is fitted with a furler. Many skippers prefer to fit very powerful jib halyard hoisters which can be tightened as wind increases. Many sailmakers make so-called 'stretch-luff' jibs which are designed to be hauled up more and more and stretched out on the luff as wind increases. Other jibs are designed to hang loose on their luff wires so that they may be stretched downwards by a Cunningham line.

With the increase in mid-boom sheeting the role of the kicking strap has become less important. Yet it is essential that either by means of a powerful kicking strap or by the intelligent use of a wide mainsheet track, twist should be eliminated as completely as possible from the mainsail when reaching and running. Theorists tell us that since wind speed and hence apparent wind angle increase with height above the water, sails should be allowed to twist off to a suitable degree. But the practical fact seems to be that all sails, if not carefully controlled, will naturally twist off far more than is needed to cope with this wind gradient effect. Hence, the twist should in practice be reduced just as far as possible. Only in survival conditions should it ever become desirable to let off the top of the sail any further. Then, when suddenly over-pressed, letting go of the kicking strap will 'dump' the wind out of the main and get the boat back upright again.

Steps in tuning

To achieve a well tuned boat work in this way:

a. Make sure your hull and foils (centreboard and rudder) are strong, light, smooth and well shaped.

b. Look to the strength and efficiency of your fittings.

c. Relate the fore and aft position of your sails to that of your hull, keel or centreboard, and rudder so that you can use a light touch on the helm.

d. Look to your rig with the principles mentioned above in mind.

e. Advance with caution. Do not be above copying others – providing those others are proven winners. Only make changes for solid reasons; work methodically; do not allow a few poor results to shake your principles and undo your gradually achieved pattern.

f. Change one thing at a time. If you have a poor memory, keep a note or log of all your changes and their observed effect in the ruling conditions of wave and wind and in the context of the competition.

If you work in this conservative, methodical, patient way, you will eventually achieve a well tuned boat. Contrary to the popular belief, there is no magic in it, nor even a rare or special ability.

12   Special Techniques

Trapezing

More boats are still kept upright by weighted keels than by crews swinging out on trapezes, but the proportion is narrowing fast. The trapeze is very much the 'in' thing. It makes the crew's job more exciting, and more rewarding.

A trapeze wire is attached to the mast at the height of the forestay, usually on each side of the mast. To lessen windage keen crews attach the trapeze wire direct to the main shroud, about 9 inches down from the shroud attachment point. The lower end of the wire must be adjustable for height. Having experimented widely with different lower end arrangements, my preference is now for a method which pulls the trapeze ring upwards, so helping to keep it in contact with the open hook on the harness (see diagram). It is possible to add a quick adjustment to the system so that the crew can alter the length to suit his harness and the day (strength of breeze, wave height, etc.), but to my mind such adjustment is not essential providing the ring fitting has two positions. Most beginners start with wires which are too short. One word of advice is that when trapezing singlehanded (as in the Contender class) the wire needs to be considerably shorter than when crewing in a two-man boat.

For crews, a correctly placed handle on the wire is extremely important. This should be at least 2 feet above the trapeze ring itself. All the best crews pull themselves out of the boat with this handle, only clipping the harness hook into the ring when already extended. This saves time when coping with the jib sheet as well. The alternative longer trapeze ring is needed when sailing downwind and the crew needs to swing aft along the gunwale to keep the bow from dipping. As a guide to correct trapeze wire length this lower ring should be some 2 inches lower than the deck. The upper ring should be about 7 inches shorter. The higher up the mast the trapeze wire is taken the easier it will be to trapeze.

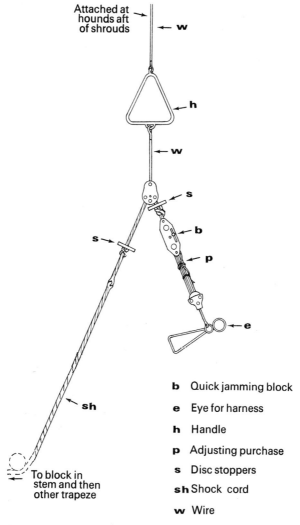

Attached at
hounds aft
of shrouds

← w

← h

← w

← s

s →

← b

← p

← e

← sh

To block in
stem and then
other trapeze

b Quick jamming block

e Eye for harness

h Handle

p Adjusting purchase

s Disc stoppers

sh Shock cord

w Wire

Trapezing systems: there are any number of ways of rigging trapeze wires, but the author and his crews have found that this one works as well as any. With the usual downward pointing hook on the harness which is fairly standard, the shock cord pulling the trapeze ring upwards holds it into the hook instead of it falling free. With the two-position ring shown here (that allows the crew to move aft off the wind) a quick adjustment purchase is not vital, but it permits variations for different crews and wind strengths. The best crews swing out holding onto the handle, clipping on later. The essential is to get out early. Harnesses are better with old fashioned lacing adjustment – the quick-action adjusting buckles nearly all slip when worn. The whole gear is pulled slightly aft in the drawing, for clarity.

One must learn to move in and out of the boat smoothly and easily, by pivoting on one bent leg and using the other as a lever. Resist the tendency to come in by hanging aft as this puts the stern down just when it should be high. The skipper should be prepared to do a lot of moving in and out himself in order that the crew can keep steady. In choppy seas, the forward leg must be well braced to resist the forward pull of the wire.

Downwind, even with a spinnaker, the skipper must learn to steer from the lee side so that his crew can stay out on the wire longer. From the wire the crew can see the spinnaker better and control it more effectively.

The crew will soon lose his fear that the wire will break. After that it is practise, practise, practise until he feels as much at home on the hook as does a monkey on a branch.

Modern trapeze harnesses have become more and more similar. Choose one with substantial reinforcement and padding in way of the hips and small of the back. Otherwise the liver and other vital organs may be painfully cramped. Be suspicious of clever, quick-fastening belts and buckles: these usually work loose with time and wear and tension. Light line lacing is usually best. The shoulder straps are vital and must be quite tight, though not so tight that one is unable to straighten out. The hook should be rigidly fastened to a substantial plate, which is always kept close to the body. Remember that when beating to windward fast and pitching into a steep sea, the ultimate strains on the system are often far greater than the body weight of the crew.

Planing

Like riding a bicycle, planing, however difficult to learn, will never afterwards be forgotten. The sensation is far too exciting. Planing is achieved first because of the potentially high power to weight ratio of the boat, second because of the strength of the wind. The third and most important factor is the skill and coordination of the crew in bringing to bear the maximum possible power.

A boat will plane earlier if she is kept flat by the crew, and if the bow is prevented from digging into the water. One has always to break over the 'hump' before skittering away over the surface of the water. The breakthrough is the difficult thing. It is achieved, as I have already hinted, by coordination. The skipper sees a puff of wind approaching. He warns his crew and as it strikes they both lunge slightly backwards. They also strike at their sheets, as if hooking a biting fish, pulling them in sharply. Perhaps the skipper will also bring his helm up slightly so that the boat bears off and the wind angle increases, although he must time this to the wave pattern.

Once the boat is up and planing, the rigging moaning, the rudder whistling and the spray hissing, it is important that sudden movements be completely avoided. If the wind heightens still more it may be necessary to ease the mainsheet, and even the jib sheet somewhat, to prevent heeling. But usually the sheets will have to be brought inboard as speed increases sharply at the start of a plane. If the wind eases the sheets may need to be struck again to give an added impetus. It may also help to luff slightly to bring the wind from further ahead and this will accelerate the apparent wind.

More and more, top small boat races are won and lost by downwind rather than upwind speed. The trend is so marked that crews are getting lighter and lighter, even at the expense of some upwind ability.

Surfing and wave riding

Closely related to planing comes surfing, or wave riding (I use the terms interchangeably). It consists of exploiting the energy of a wave to increase the speed of your boat. In British waters opportunities for this grand sport are pretty circumscribed and hence we are not so good at it as our cousins in Australia, California and elsewhere. A good planer makes a good surfer. The two things demand the same sensitivity, the same quick, almost instinctive judgments.

Since you will want to stay on a wave for as long as possible it will be best to run across at an angle instead of at right angles to the breaking edge. This, of course, is what board surfers do. Often it helps to move weight forward, but unless one is very skilled, fore and aft weight shifting will almost always end up with the weight being moved at precisely the wrong time. A wave is caught as the bow digs into it, either when the wave has rolled up from behind or when it has, more rarely, already caught up. Some waves are best held by luffing and others by bearing off; it almost never pays to stay put. As speed increases sheets must be brought in smartly. To encourage a surf it often pays to strike the sheets hard, but one must be careful not to break the racing rule against pumping and ooching.

Big yachts may be made to surf, but as with all big boat operations, comes about with less crew participation.

Surfing is even more fun than planing – and that's saying something!

Ghosting

Some people – and by no means always those who are best at planing – have the ability to generate speed in near calm conditions and to get their boat moving at 2 or 3 knots while others are apparently completely becalmed with sails hanging dead as hung stoats. You need stealth, patience, stillness, good eyesight, and even the smoke from a cigarette will do no harm, externally, at any rate.

Trim the boat by the bow and move the weight to leeward to cause a heel and help the sails drop into shape. Forget all the usual rules about the normal sheet tensions and angles and let everything out further than you would believe possible. Ease away on outhauls and halyards. Get the sails loose and try to stay loose yourself. Don't worry too much about pointing high; concentrate only on starting the boat moving through the water. Once you have a little momentum then, and only then, should you begin to think about pointing up a bit and pulling in the sheets. The modern boat can be made to sail in a wind which is moving slower than a walking pace. But things will not begin to happen until boat and sails are still and the latter falling into their natural shape. Keep helm alterations to a minimum; resist the impulse to tack on headers until they are well established. Never give up or sit back and relax and throw up your hands as if it is all farcical. The race committee will decide that soon enough and call you in if it really is farcical but this doesn't often happen.

The best training ground for near-calm sailing is in smooth, tide-free waters. Around British coasts, tides are often so strong that courses cannot be completed unless boats are moving at several knots, but on lakes and non-tidal waters it is possible to discover how you can build up speed bit by bit, in very little wind at all.

Sailing backwards

This is not as stupid as it sounds: the ability to be able to sail backwards – sometimes known as taking a sternboard – is more valuable now than ever. There are two distinct reasons. One is that the modern keelboat, with her steep, deep fin keel and rudder blade, is particularly likely to accumulate weed on these underwater appendages. The best way I know of ridding the boat of this weed is to take a sternboard shortly before starting. The other possible use is when one finds oneself heading early for the starting line without time or elbow room for a complete turnaround and restart, or when, in a very large start, one finds oneself carried too close to the line before gunfire.

To take a sternboard, or sail backwards, first luff gradually head to wind. Let the jib sheet fly, then have a crew member push out the main boom on the old lee side. The sail will fill inside out, as it were, pressing itself against the crewman. Providing he can hold on, the boat will now begin to move astern. She will show a marked desire to turn which must be met by prompt movement of the rudder, remembering that tiller direction must now be reversed. Since the action of backing the main will make the boat want to tack (as seen from the tack on which she was sailing before the luff) it will normally be necessary to push the tiller down as she gains speed astern. Then as she picks up way it will be necessary to centre the tiller. You will soon find yourself making several knots astern. Weed should detach itself in the first few boats' lengths but take a little more time to ensure that any weed falling from the rudder gets a chance to drop free from the keel as well. As for manoeuvring just short of the starting line, one would hardly ever want to take a full blooded sternboard since one would presumably have to keep well clear of those coming up from behind. But the boat's forward motion can be arrested very quickly by backing the mainsail by thrusting the boom out against the wind while the boat is still on a tack (but pointing very high, otherwise it will be difficult to get the backed main to fill). If you come all the way up into the wind, you will find the boat difficult to control in the confined space which will usually be yours. From personal experience I know that a small quantity of weed the size of a hand nail brush, can significantly slow a boat the size of a Star if it is snagged at the top of the forward edge of the fin keel!

When racing there will not be any time to take a sternboard and any weed collected during the race will have to be removed in another way. In boats of under 30 feet weed should be removable with a long, thin bamboo (but it must be stiff enough not to bend much when put into the water). Usually, once weed is touched by the bamboo, it will start sliding down until it drops off the keel bottom (there is usually a marked downward trend of the water flowing past the leading·edge). Sailing my Tempest in the weedy waters of Brittany, we developed a technique in which the crew used the bamboo from his trapeze, thrusting it deep in the water ahead of the fin and then letting if fall back against the hull. After the fin was clear, the bamboo was handed to me to clear the rudder.

It is hardly necessary to say that weed may be cleared from centreboards by partially raising the board and rudder blade. This may be necessary on every leg of the course in weedy conditions. Weed normally floats, so will be picked up by the keel or rudder close under the hull, where it causes most drag.

Windward heeling

It has often been shown that boats will run faster downwind if allowed to heel slightly to windward. The reason is twofold: by heeling the boat over, the mainsail area comes more nearly over the keel and therefore hull balance is improved and less rudder is needed to correct incipient weather helm (though this will apply mainly to boats without spinnakers and most of all to single-sail boats). Second, with the fat modern type of hull a windward heel will induce hull imbalance and consequent lee helm which will cancel out the aforementioned tendency of the sail area, to leeward, trying to weather-cock the hull.

Usually a few degrees (not more than 10) of heel will suffice. Many OK, Optimist and Finn sailors overdo it and heel to weather far too much. It is worth thinking about in all craft, no matter how large, for even though their spinnakers may be much larger than their mainsails, the axis of the spinnaker will be to leeward.

Wool tufting

This isn't a technique so much as a helpful aid to better sailing. But it doesn't seem to belong in any other chapter of this book. I am referring to the modern practice of affixing wool tufts, each some 8 inches long, to the forepart of a headsail and about 10 per cent of sail width aft of the luff, on both sides of the sail.

These tufts serve as valuable guides in telling whether the boat is sailing too high or too low, or whether the jib itself is trimmed too hard or too slack. When the sail is well trimmed and the boat is on the right windward heading, both windward and leeward tufts will flow smoothly aft and lie horizontal. If one sails too high and pinches, the weather side tufts will normally lift from the sail and begin to jump around. If sailing too far offwind the lee tuft will also begin to act up in this way. The point is that whenever one or both tufts are breaking away, you know that your heading or sheeting is incorrect.

Some people fit several pairs of tufts at about 4 foot intervals, one set above the other. But it is difficult to watch more than one pair at once, and I would recommend one pair only, fitted about one-quarter of the luff length up from the bottom.

Some people apply thin oil to the sailcloth in way of the tufts with the idea of making the fabric more translucent so that the lee one may be more easily seen, but usually with thin fabrics and good sunlight this is unnecessary. Use dark wool which is more easily seen.

231

Sailing to windward with wool tufts, one feels something of a cheat, as if one had switched on the automatic pilot. Nonetheless, these tufts are absolutely legal and I have seen near-beginners using them and steering their boat to windward far better than they would otherwise have done. And I do know of at least one World Champion calibre sailor (Glen Foster of New York) who would never be without them.

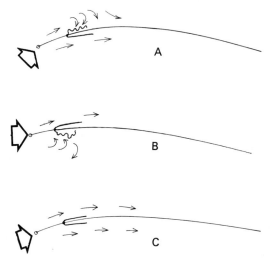

Wool tufts fitted to a jib can be of great value in showing whether your jib is sheeted correctly and if you are sailing the correct course relative to the wind. Some experts, such as Tempest world champion Glen Foster of the USA are never without them. (A) is too much off the wind, (B) is pinching, (C) everything is just right.

One might add, parenthetically, that the conventional rectangular racing flag is far from being the best means of detecting wind direction. Far better to replace the flag with one of the proprietary arrow type wind vanes, preferably the ones which also have tacking indicators. These, being balanced, are much more sensitive and accurate although liable to damage when raising and lowering the mast. Note that the British RYA racing rules require a racing boat to fly a rectangular flag, while the world-wide IYRU rules do not call for such a thing. The RYA rule may be met by attaching a small rectangle of cloth to the leech of the mainsail, just below the headboard.

False tacking

There will be certain situations when it becomes vital to escape the close cover of another competitor. Maybe it is a team race and his covering is slowing both of you while, more important, allowing a teammate of his to catch and pass both of you. Perhaps it is a two-boat match race and you simply have to beat him somehow.

Whatever the reason, if you find that he is able to match every tack, every wriggle, with one of his own, so that you, far from breaking through are only dropping further back, the time has come to try a false tack. After a rapid rally of real tacks you noisily come head to wind and free your sheets again, but instead of turning right through the wind and actually falling away on the other tack, you fall back eventually onto the old tack and resume it. If the manoeuvre has been well timed, you will see, out of the corner of your eye, that your erstwhile coverer, in his eagerness, went all the way and tacked fully.

You have now split tacks with him. If he tries to cover and swings back to your original tack once again, he is bound to kill his speed and possibly end up dead in the water. If he doesn't do this you will have the advantage of a clear wind while he has lost initiative. You must use the ruse sparingly, for your opponent will also know it, and if he lets you go head to wind and back again, while he simply holds his course, he will end up by gaining distance on you. It is, of course, essential to take the whole crew into one's confidence.

Kedging

In light airs and strong currents, especially when racing off-shore, enormous comparative distances may be won against rivals, even though you don't move ahead at all. This is because you have alertly anchored to prevent the tide from taking you backwards, while backwards go all the others.

Kedge anchors should be much smaller than main or bower anchors and on small craft can have very thin, light (but long) lines. If they are light they can be speedily fetched, used and just as quickly recovered.

What is needed is an alert navigator or a skipper who can quickly decide whether he is gaining or losing over the ground (as opposed to moving through the water). This is not nearly as easy as it may sound, particularly when sailing in bad visibility, or out of sight of land or at night.

Kedges are also of great use in inshore racing, especially in such strongly tidal waters as the Solent. Very often races are started with the entire fleet kedged. Usually, in these conditions, a down-tide start is given so that at least the class will be taken away from the line and space left for the next class. The technique here is to anchor before the start, carefully planning the best position. Sometimes the kedge is run out from the stern, so that the boat is facing in the correct direction, but beware lest a growing breeze makes recovery difficult. It can help to take the line to an unused sheet winch in a keelboat. Always give a kedge plenty of line, more than three times the depth of water. Otherwise the light line will pull straight and prevent the light anchor from digging in. Use your seamanship and common sense to prevent your line becoming crossed with others.

The artful dodger can actually gain distance, when the time comes to haul up his kedge, by taking a sheer as the anchor is brought up.

Conclusion

Anchoring may seem to be an odd way of winning a race, but as you should have gathered from all that you have now read, sailing races are not often won by dashing fastest in a straight line. And herein lies the fascination of a very great sport that more and more people are happily discovering.

It's a subtle art and an opportunist one, and best of all it offers infinite variety. No one race is quite the same as any other. No man will ever learn all the answers to all the possible permutations of wind, water, boat and sail. So prepare with care, practise like mad, race as often as possible and make sure you let none of your hard-won experience slip through your fingers – and at the end of all that, hope for the best.